Blood
on the
Tracks

Dylan's masterpiece in blue

To Marga

Time is a jet plane, it moves too fast

Contents

I'm not a big Dylan fan. I've got *Blonde On Blonde* and *Highway 61 Revisited,* obviously. And *Bringing It All Back Home* and *Blood On the Tracks.* Anyone who likes music owns those four.

- Nick Hornby, *31 Songs,* 2003

Prithee, look back, there's blood on the track

Already in the first English translation of Grimm's Fairy Tales, 1823 by Edgar Taylor, the bloody, cruel originals are watered down. Later, in the twentieth century the edifying theories of influential child psychologists like Bruno Bettelheim and especially the cutifying treatments by Disney, threaten the horror content of the source texts.

These source texts are the fairy tales as collected and recorded by Jakob and Wilhelm Grimm in the beginning of the nineteenth century. In *Kinder- und Hausmärchen* (1812) the blood splatters against the walls, the evil undergoes the most lugubrious punishments and we do not care about a few corpses less or more. The feet of Cinderella's step-sisters, for example, are fairly spared in Taylor's translation. The first step sister has to sacrifice only one toe to fit in the shoe ("So the silly girl cut off her toe"), and the second step sister gets the foot wrung into the shoe by her angry stepmother with bare hands – although, granted, some blood flows (*"But her mother squeezed it in till the blood came"*).

The Grimm Brothers do not worry about the delicate children's souls. Without any fuss the first daughter's toes are all cut off and equally resolutely number two's heel is chopped off — at any cost one of them has to fit in that shoe. Plus, in Grimm's version the ladies are severely punished, too. Driven by opportunism, the vicious stepsisters limp into the wedding-party of Cinderella and her prince on the last page. They soon regret it; the pigeons attack both shrews and peck out their eyes.

But Taylor insipidly confines himself to one single toe, deletes that gruesome ending altogether and puts an end to the fairy tale well before the wedding, when the prince leaves Cinderella's home for the third time, this time with the right bride behind him on his horse. In other translations and adaptations, it gets even sweeter; Cinderella forgives her stepsisters and on the wedding ball they are coupled to two distinguished gentlemen.

Halfway through the twentieth century, translators E.V. Lucas, Lucy Crane and Marian Edwards return to the blood and the horror, and they get away with it. Some poetic liberties on their return to the source the ladies still grant themselves. In the rhyme that the birds chirp to warn the prince against deception, for instance. Twice the prince rides with a wrong bride past the hazel with Cinderella's feathered friends, and both times the pigeons call:

> Rucke di guck, rucke di guck,
> Blut ist im Schuck:
> der Schuck ist zu klein,
> die rechte Braut sitzt noch daheim.

To the first translator, Edgar Taylor, that is way too scary and he composes bloodlessly:

Back again! back again! look to the shoe!
The shoe is too small, and not made for you!
Prince! prince! look again for thy bride,
For she's not the true one that sits by thy side

But later, the female trio translators is not that anxious and almost literally interprets:

Prithee, look back, prithee, look back,
there's blood on the track.
The shoe is too small;
at home, the true bride is waiting thy call

This translation, with illustrations by Fritz Kredel, hits the American market in 1945 and is an instant sales success. Not very surprising; after the Bible, *Kinder- und Hausmärchen* is the best-selling book of all time. On the bookshelf in Woodstock, where the young family of Bob and Sara Dylan lives, is probably the reprint from 1965.

To the puzzlers who think *Blood On The Tracks* is the Big Ultimate Dylan Divorce and Heartbreak Album, the similarity between the Cinderella quote and the title of the album is attractive. The blood on the path represents that the prince is on the way with the wrong maiden and that he must get rid of her. Bingo, these exegetes think. By 1974 Bob Dylan reaches the conclusion that his marriage with Sara is on a dead end, he lays his soul on the table in songs like "Simple Twist Of Fate", "You're A Big Girl Now" and especially "Idiot Wind " and calls the album *I Am On The Road With The Wrong Woman*.

The popular, widespread notion that *Blood On The Tracks* is autobiographical and thematises the dilapidated state of his marriage, annoys Dylan. He admits early, in a radio interview with Mary Travers (Mary from Peter, Paul and Mary) in April '75, that the songs express pain. In his own words, he is surprised that people enjoy the album so much: "It's hard for me to relate to that. I mean, you know, people enjoying the type of pain, you know." And there is the first defensive reaction, when Travers half-heartedly suggests that it could be autobiographical:

> MT: Well, perhaps maybe the word "enjoy" is the wrong word. Maybe a better word is to say that you're moved. I was moved by the album. You know, there were things that I could relate to in that album that grew as sense to me. You made sense to me on that album. I felt that it was a much more, well, for me, I felt it was much more "first person" as opposed to third person.
> BD: Well, it makes it more clearly defined, but it still doesn't necessarily make it any better than, than, doing it, 'cause you can do it in second, third, fourth person too, you know, it's all the same, sure it is. Um. I know what you mean though.

Not quite coherent (the 'fourth person' does not exist, not in any grammar), but the drift of Dylan's reply is clear: whenever an 'I' speaks, you may also fill in a 'you' or a 'he', that does not make any difference. And implicitly: this is not about me, Bob Dylan. *Je est un autre*, says Rimbaud, and Dylan fully subscribes to that statement, also in so many words, in his autobiography *Chronicles* ("When I read those words the bells went off").

On the other hand, the bard provides ammunition more than once, especially in interviews with journalists with whom he seems to feel at ease. As with Craig McGregor, March 1978 in Australia:

> CM: I meant more, you write songs about Sara – I wonder
> whether you can channel your private emotions into your
> music, that's one of the reasons you're able to write songs. You
> suffer, and that comes out into your songs.
> BD: (*Pause*) That particular song, well... some songs you figure
> you're better off not to have written. There's a few of them
> layin' around.

Initially the men talk about the closing song of Desire, about "Sara", the song of which Dylan at other times asserts with dry eyes that it is not about Sara, but here Dylan admits almost carelessly that it happens to him more than once - that he incorporates his own experiences and private feelings into his songs.

In the years that follow, Dylan grows increasingly assertive and explicit when confronted with the interpretation that the album is about himself and his marital affairs. This culminates in the booklet in the *Biograph* collection box (1985), in which he even starts cursing: these 'fools', these 'stupid and misleading jerks' who, with their 'unimaginative mentality' think that it is about him and his wife. After that he again asserts that he does not write *confessional songs*.

He does not convince the Dylanologists. And his son Jakob does not make it easier in an interview, May 2005 with Anthony DeCurtis for The New York Times:

> "When I'm listening to "Subterranean Homesick Blues," I'm
> grooving along just like you. But when I'm listening to "Blood on
> the Tracks," that's about my parents."

Words that resonate, in the Dylan community, and still Jakob's most quoted words. But it is not entirely pure. In the process of the quotation being eagerly pumped around, this 'proof' that *Blood On The Tracks* indeed ís autobiographical, the nuance is lost that it is an indirect quotation. It is true that it is printed in that interview with Jakob, but precisely this quote only appears in an intermezzo in which journalist DeCurtis notes what Andrew Slater, the former manager of Jakob's band The Wallflowers, has told him about what Jakob supposedly said years earlier. It is hearsay, not words that the journalist has recorded from the mouth of Jakob Dylan.

If we assume that *Blood On The Tracks* is not an encrypted, indiscrete ego document, the question about the title will remain open. Very open; the word *track* has four or five different meanings, each one opening a new range of interpretation possibilities.

Dylan's fascination for trains suggests that he himself thinks of the meaning 'rails, train track' when using the word *tracks*. From his first album on, it is a coming and going of trains, tramps walking along the tracks, conductors, wagons, steam whistles and stations. In the roughly three hundred songs that Dylan wrote before *Blood On The Tracks*, thirty trains pass by and there are as many train-related references (station master, down the line, coachman, railroad tracks, railroad men, railroad gate and railroad gin, to name a few), so Dylan's self-reflection in the radio interview with Elliot Mintz, 1991, does have some ground: "That's just my hang up, you know, trains."

Chekhov might be a clue, on condition that we take Dylan's hint from Chronicles seriously:

> Eventually I would even record an entire album based on Chekhov short stories - critics thought it was autobiographical - that was fine.

The most famous Blood On The Train Tracks is the blood of Anna Karenina. But alas; that is Tolstoy, and neither does it flow in a short story. In Chekhov's work dozens of trains pass by, but apart from a single reference in an insignificant sideline, never with bloody consequences. And that one referral is once again based on the tragic fate of the unfortunate Anna Karenina (in *The Duel*, 1891).

But then again, Dylan has of course built a solid reputation of screwing up the names of writers and their works. In *Chronicles*, for example, he mentions Pericles' *Ideal State Of Democracy* (the statesman and general Pericles did not write books at all) and he casually cites "Sophocles' book on the nature and function of the gods" – in reality Sophocles only wrote tragedies. And likewise in interviews we come across such, intentional or unintentional, slips. As in the same interview with Craig McGregor (New Musical Express), in March 1978:

> CM: Listening to Tangled Up In Blue, I got the feeling it's like an autobiography; a sort of funny, wry, compressed novel...
> BD: Yeah, that's the first I ever wrote that I felt free enough to change all the... what is it, the tenses around, is that what it is?
> CM: The person...
> BD: The he and the she and the I and the you, and the we and the us – I figured it was all the same anyway – I could throw them all in where they floated right - and it works on that level.

CM: It's got those nice lines at the end, about "*There was music in the cafés at night / And revolution in the air*" and "*Some are mathematicians, some are carpenters wives / I don't know how it all got started, I don't know / what they do with their lives.*"
BD: I like that song. Yeah, that poet from the 13th century.
CM: Who was that?
BD: Plutarch. Is that his name?

True, Plutarch sometimes resides in Rome, becomes a Roman citizen in later years and is known by his Latin name, but: he is a Greek and lives in the *first* century. Even the job title 'poet' is not correct; Plutarch does not write poems, but biographies and philosophical essays, in Greek, by the way. With that malapropism, Dylan at the same time puts into perspective the research of the descriptors that scroll back and forth in the works of Dante and Petrarch (who live in the *four*teenth century, really) to find a line to "Tangled Up In Blue". Matching the atmosphere of the song and the words *And every one of them words rang true / And glowed like burnin' coal* sooner brings Boccaccio to mind, actually, but just as little luck there: wrong century again (1313-1375).

Inaccuracies and false scents enough, all in all, to not take Dylan's own reference to 'the short stories of Chekhov' too literally. He could just as well have meant 'Russian literature from previous centuries' or 'Tolstoy', and therefore the album title could have been inspired by the reading of *Anna Karenina*. Not entirely incongruous; Anna's jump before the train is driven by frustrated love and jealousy, two leading motifs in the songs on *Blood On The Tracks*.

A third meaning of *tracks* is grist to the mill to a poet who, according to Joan Baez, is 'so good at keeping things vague': *album tracks*, the individual songs on a record. With this semantic charge, Dylan uses the word *track* just as often meaning 'song'; in *Chronicles* alone, he means eight times 'song recording' when he writes *a track*, and in the published interviews we also encounter it dozens of times as a synonym for 'song'.

In that case *Blood On The Tracks* becomes something like 'there is blood in these songs, my heart and soul lie in these songs', which of course is a welcome interpretation for the autobiographical signifiers.

Not at all unambiguous, all in all, this polysemic album title. Considering the long list of Dylan's album titles, the poetic vagueness of a title like *Blood On The Tracks* is not necessarily a trademark of the bard, but it is not exceptional either. We know that since his fifth album, *Bringing It All Back Home* (1965), Dylan is allowed to come up with the titles himself (until that time the boys and girls from CBS' marketing department consider it their task) and we know that Dylan cares:

> Well, I always like to tie the name of the album in with some song. Or if not some song, some kind of general feeling. I think that just about fit because it was less in the way, and less specific than any of the other ones there. Certainly couldn't call the album *Lay Lady Lay*. I wouldn't have wanted to call it that, although that name was brought up. It didn't get my vote, but it was brought up.
>
> (*Rolling Stone* interview, november 1969)

Since 1965, Dylan has recorded about 30 official, regular studio albums and given them a name. Half of them are linked to a song title (*Highway 61 Revisited, Slow Train Coming, Tempest*), some names indeed express a traceable 'general feeling' (*Self Portrait, Bringing It All Back Home*) and with a dozen titles Dylan is admittedly 'less specific', but the title is still 'in the way', the chosen title is an extra challenge to interpret the album and the songs. *Blonde On Blonde* is the first example and in the 70s Dylan succumbs three times for the temptation to put an alienating, misty icing on the cake: *Desire, Street Legal* and this *Blood On The Tracks*.

Despite this mistiness, the word combination gradually penetrates the public's collective memory. A British collection of stories about criminal activities on the railroad is called *Blood On The Tracks* (David Brandon and Alan Brooke, 2017), as well as the first episode of *Unravel*, an Australian podcast by investigative journalists on unsolved crimes (2018), the first thriller in the *Sidney Rose Parnell* series by writer Barbara Nickless (2016), the fifteenth episode of the TV series *Werewolf* (1987), various artworks by musicians, painters and sculptors, research reports by molecular biologists and medical specialists, an episode from the game version of *Guardians Of The Galaxy*, and so on. Brian S. Willson, the Vietnam veteran and peace activist who, in a demonstration on the tracks in front of a munitions transport, remains demonstratively seated, gets run over and loses both legs in 1987, shows a macabre sort of mental toughness by calling his memoirs *Blood On The Tracks* (2011).

The title is, in short, starting to get disengaged from Dylan's masterpiece. The fanatical teenagers who chase the *Silver Blood On The Tracks Trophy* in the *Tell-Tale Series* of the *Guardians* game at their Xbox will largely be unfamiliar with "Idiot Wind". The zealous cell biology students who plough through their professor's neuroscientific study, *Blood On The Tracks* by Konstantinos Meletis, 2003, probably will not be able to sing along with "Buckets Of Rain".

But that the timeless masterpiece of the Nobel Prize winner will cross their paths sooner or later, is certain. That does not take more than a simple twist of fate.

1   Tangled Up In Blue

It is an anecdote that Leonard Cohen likes to tell, apparently, for it can be read in many interviews. It refers to his late magnum opus, the wonderful song "Hallelujah", the song that surprisingly but gradually climbed up from little-noticed album track (on *Various Positions*, 1984) to a classic, to one of his most loved and most covered (more than three hundred versions) songs.

That triumphal march begins in 1991, when John Cale wants to do the song for the tribute album *I'm Your Fan*. Cale notices at a concert that Cohen sings different words than on the record and he asks the Canadian for the correct lyrics. Cohen, who by his own account never could finish the song and would write over eighty couplets, faxes fifteen couplets.

Cale picks out five of them. "It was a long roll of fax paper. And then I chose whichever ones were really *me*. Some of them were religious and coming out of my mouth would have been a little difficult to believe. I chose the cheeky ones." This variant is picked up by Jeff Buckley, who records an unforgettable version for his first and only album, *Grace* from 1994. Ten years after his death in 1997, it is released as a single, after being included in Rolling Stone's list of *The Greatest Songs Of All Time* (in 2004, at 259).

But Dylan deserves the credit for recognizing the greatness of the song much earlier. He sings "Hallelujah" as early as July 8, 1988, in Cohen's hometown of Montreal and again a few weeks later, in Los Angeles. The men have known and appreciated each other for a long time, but this really flatters Cohen, which is why he brings it up regularly, in various interviews.

> "That was a song that took me a long time to write. Dylan and I were having coffee the day after his concert in Paris a few years ago and he was doing that song in concert. And he asked me how long it took to write it. And I told him a couple of years. I lied actually. It was more than a couple of years.
> Then I praised a song of his, "I and I", and asked him how long it had taken, and he said, 'Fifteen minutes.' [*Laughter*]"

It is true, there are many testimonies from bystanders who tell that Dylan so phenomenally fast dashes off song lyrics. George Harrison says that Dylan produces the world hit "Handle With Care" in a few minutes, close comrades-in-arms like Al Kooper, Kevin Odegard and Duke Robillard have throughout the decades all completely similar memories of a Dylan who, in between studio turbulence, card-playing musicians and tea ladies, aside at a coffee table quickly adds a verse or writes a complete song lyric, but still: Leonard Cohen inquires after the wrong song.

He should have asked about "Tangled Up In Blue". That is the song that according to Dylan took him two years to write and ten years to live, and thereby he refers to his years of marriage with Sara Lownds.

"Tangled Up In Blue" opens *Blood On The Tracks* (1975), the record that, rightly or wrongly, is considered the most beautiful divorce record in pop history, and one of Dylan's Great Masterpieces. Most of the lyrics on this album are poignant, moving, poetic and sometimes painfully clear, but this highly acclaimed *Tangled* is far from unambiguous.

This lack of clarity is first of all caused by the confusing use of personal pronouns (the nameless *I*, *She* and *He*) and secondly by the inconsistency in time, which leads to an ardent puzzling, cutting and pasting of interpreters in order to find a linear narrative. Verse sequence 3-4-5-6-1-2-7 then provides, with some inching, squeezing and pinching, a more or less coherent rise and fall of a love story. Other exegetes quote Dylan's own words:

"I wanted to defy time, so that the story took place in the present and past at the same time. When you look at a painting, you can see any part of it or see all of it together. I wanted that song to be like a painting."

Well, that does shed some light. "Tangled Up In Blue" poetically tells us that the storms of life leave their marks and that we are becoming a different person along the way. Dylan rightly chooses the collage technique and gives sufficient hints to justify a biographical interpretation. Sara was not only a model but also Playboy bunny (*She was workin' 'in a topless place*), and indeed still married when they first met. In his early years Dylan sometimes plays in a joint on *Montague Street* and he lives with a couple in the neighbourhood, he is originally from Minnesota (*the Great North Woods*) and recalls his *Girl From The North Country*. For the title explanation, Dylan has also lifted a more prosaic tip of the veil: to the journalist Ron Rosenbaum he reveals that he wrote the song after having immersed himself in the music of Joni Mitchell's *Blue* for a weekend.

One could go on like this for a while, but it is not all too relevant for the lyrical power of this song. Dylan the Poet expresses here how this protagonist's life too is defined by the oldest cliché, how a life can be summarised in the three words Searching For Love – *love is all there is*, as he sang a few years earlier. You find love, you lose it, and you go on. *Keep on keepin' on, headin' for another joint.*

To make it even more difficult for the Dylan interpreters: there is no song in his catalogue with which Dylan has scraped and tinkered so much. In September 1974 he records the first two versions, which still are largely told in the third person. There are some small textual differences between the two versions, the first version is ultimately chosen for the LP. Dylan then stays with his family in the North over Christmas. He shares the recordings from New York, a few hours before the records will be pressed, and brother David expresses concerns. Dylan agrees and re-records five songs with local musicians. *Tangled* receives the most radical make-over on all fronts (different keys, different instrumentation, tempo), and, by extension, also lyrically. That version is released on *Blood On The Tracks*.

In the following years, Dylan continues to rewrite and ultimately declares the 80s version (to be heard on *Real Live* from 1984) the final. Hardly any line is maintained in this re-issue. That is not the only clue to reveal Dylan's own fascination; to this day the song belongs to his most performed. On the list of indefatigable Dylan watcher Olof Björner from Sweden it occupies the fourth place for years now, with more than a thousand performances, after "All Along The Watchtower", "Like A Rolling Stone" and "Highway 61 Revisited". Björner's painstaking monk's work registers all official concert performances since 1958. Statistically, *Tangled* should actually even rank a bit higher; the first fifteen songs on that list are, except for *Tangled*, all written between 1963 and 1968, and thus have a lead of up to twelve years. A "Blowin' In The Wind", for example, is twelve years older, but since long has been taken over – Dylan has sung "Tangled Up In Blue" over a hundred times more often than that monument.

And it does not stop there, Dylan's own fascination. In his wonderful book *Why Dylan Matters*, Harvard professor Richard F. Thomas points out the return of the image of the *waitress* in 1997, in the overwhelming song "Highlands" on *Time Out Of Mind*. In the alienating intermezzo halfway through the song, in those seven couplets that create a kind of one-act play for two in an empty restaurant in Boston, we recognize the male protagonist from "Tangled Up In Blue". He is in the "wrong time", he *picked the wrong time to come*, says the waitress, who has thrown him back in time through her looks and behaviour, back to 1974.

Just like her predecessor, she carefully studies the restaurant guest (*She studied the lines on my face* vs. *She studied me closely*), we are back in an empty catering facility and when he draws her portrait at her insistence, he must strangely enough draw it from memory, although she is still standing in front of him. There is absolutely no resemblance, she says a moment later, throwing the drawing back at him. On the contrary, the satisfied artist speaks to her, there most certainly is – after all, he has made a lifelike portrait of that waitress in that *topless place*. The final verse, when the waitress asks which female authors he has read, illustrates once again that the narrator is in a different time zone. "Erica Jong," he answers triumphantly. Jong's controversial *Fear Of Flying* is from 1973.

Fellow musicians share Dylan's enthusiasm for the song. There are more than a hundred cover versions in circulation, but here too, more than ever, is the harsh truth: it is not easy to step out of the master's shadow. Most artists fail to hold the tension, the urgency – if the artist, like Dylan, colours the seven couplets in the same way seven times, then it does require some mastery to avoid tediousness. Only the master craftsman is able to restrict himself, as Goethe taught, and here too only a few remain standing. Jerry Garcia, Dickey Betts and especially a remarkable Ben Sidran (*Dylan Different*, 2009) are doing very well.

The best cover though, by far, is from the Indigo Girls, on their live album *1200 Curfew* (1995). Particularly respectful and lovingly executed, with a beautiful progression in the arrangement, tastefully dosed singing together and a very successful turnaround in rhythm and orchestration in the sixth verse (*I lived with them on Montague Street*) – they most certainly do not restrict themselves. And right they are.

Leonard Cohen never dared to. In 1985 "Tangled Up In Blue" is number two in his personal top five, as can be learned from the book *In His Own Words* by the devout Cohen fan Jim Devlin (number one is Ray Charles' "Take These Chains From My Heart") and the song is untouchable. Cohen often and heartily professes his awe for Dylan's masterpiece, but not on stage. In interviews, yes. And majestic, poetic actually, is his commentary on Dylan's Nobel Prize: *It's like pinning a medal on Mount Everest for being the highest mountain.*

2   Simple Twist Of Fate

An older couple strolls through a park in Rome, when the man is suddenly struck by a shocking insight: he does not love his wife at all. He shares this awareness with her, but it does not impress her that much – she stopped loving him long ago. "So you want to get divorced," she deduces, undisturbed, and swiftly settles the necessities. "Give me money for the rest of the holiday and off you go." Insecurely, the man obeys. But he does not feel liberated. Hours later he is still sitting in the dark on an ancient stone in the Colosseum, still a bit dazed. Perhaps it was all *A Little Too Sudden*, as the 1977 short story of Herman Pieter de Boer is called. It can be found in the collection *De Kellnerin*.

The Rotterdam writer is inspired here by one of the many possible perspectives of "Simple Twist Of Fate": the song can be understood as the swan song of an extinct love, a description of the physical breaking point, the point where the lovers actually part. The song does not let him go, hereafter. In 1983 De Boer writes the hit "Annabel" for Hans de Booij (top 5 in Belgium and The Netherlands) and this time he chooses another, more popular scenario: too late, the man realises that the one-night stand who just left was probably the love of his life ("But two hours later I was still awake, lying on my back").

Also possible. Just like her big sister, "Tangled Up In Blue", *Simple Twist* is not only ambiguous, but constantly on the move, too. The words change per performance, Dylan swaps personal pronouns, sometimes pushes the text in one direction (and then suggests that the lady's love is paid for:

> *She raised her weary head and couldn't help but hate*
> *Cashing in on a simple twist of fate*),

Then in another direction, when he reveals that the woman is called "Suze" (*I remember Suze and the way she talked*, June '81 in London), the hotel where that last (or first and only) night is consumed, is a *strange* hotel, a *riverfront* hotel, *cheap*, *renovated* and *little*, and sometimes gets a name: *Grand Hotel*, *Rio Grande Hotel* and *Sainte Claire Hotel*. The latter, by the way, being a notorious haunted hotel in San Jose - a strange hotel indeed.

It could be argued that the song, at least in its original design, was written with the first great love Suze Rotolo in mind. The subtitle in that sketching stage is "Fourth Street Affair" and that is not very cryptic – it refers to the apartment in which he and Suze live until August '63, 161 West 4th Street. The reverie in the autobiography *Chronicles*, that Suze might have been his spiritual soul mate, lays out a second line ("I still believe she was my twin") and it is also remarkable that Dylan uses the word *fate* here, when he records his memory of the end of the relationship with Rotolo: "Eventually fate flagged it down and it came to a full stop".

It does not affect the strength of the poem, of course. Even with all those text changes, hardly any loss of quality occurs. The first verse and the perspective shift of the last verse are maintained, as is the walk along the old canal, and that is sufficient, apparently; many roads lead to Rome.

Joan Baez, the first person to record a cover (on *Diamonds And Rust*, 1975), stands out because of her good-natured, very witty imitation of Dylan's vocal style in the fourth verse, but also by fiddling around with the lyrics. Joan does not like parrots, that much is evident by now. When she ventures into Donovan's "Legend Of The Girl Child Linda" (1967) together with her sister Mimi and Judy Collins, she mixes up the verses, gulls and doves are allowed to stay, but the verse with the parrot, *where parrots are talking their words with such ease*, has disappeared.

In retrospect, the parrot allergy is apparent already in 1965, when Baez is very lucky that Dylan throws her "Farewell Angelina". Since 1991, since *The Bootleg Series 1-3*, we know for certain that Joan has also rejected verses from that song: yes indeed, the verse with *the camouflaged parrot*. And the only other parrot in Dylan's oeuvre, the one that emerges in "Simple Twist Of Fate", Baez now also sneaky eliminates. Due to the comical parody of Dylan's nasal vocal style in the fifth verse, it is hardly noticeable that she cunningly changes that original line of text *and walks along with a parrot that talks* into *small waves whisper to the rocks*.

The origin of the aversion is unclear. In her autobiography *And A Voice To Sing With*, Baez lavishly dwells on her illnesses, neuroses and anxieties, but she never once mentions psittacosis or ornithophobia

Furthermore, the saxophone does not play in the distance, but "somewhere nearby" and the revision of the last verse seems to be a model for the later versions by the master himself:

> *People tell me it's a crime*
> *To feel too much at any one time*
> *All it cost me was a dime but the bells refuse to ring*
> *He was born in the spring but I was born too late*
> *Blame it on a simple twist of fate*

The Literals will be pleased with the gender change. Finally, the birth *in the spring* is "right" (Dylan was indeed born in the spring – Suze, Sara and Joan are all *born too late*, in autumn and winter).

But it is, as Dylan says in the radio interview with Paul Vincent (San Francisco 1980), not detrimental, not decisive for the content of the song. Nor for the beauty. Far more decisive is the classical form. In these days, the poet Dylan is rather addicted to his own version of an antique ballad form inspired by François Villon (1431-1463), recognisable by the repetition of a single line at the end of each stanza. On *Blood On The Tracks* he chooses this form for five of the ten songs (in *Tangled, You're Gonna Make Me Lonesome, Shelter* and *Jack Of Hearts*) and also the outtake "Up To Me" is written around such a recurring verse.

The music is gorgeous. Simple enough, that descending melody line, but the fusion with the text is a brilliant find. It gives a magical sparkle to the rhyme scheme that on paper almost looks like an everyday rhyme (*a a a b b c c*). The sparse use of the minor chord is masterful too. Everyone else would, given the melancholic lyrics, play the entire song in minor. Song Maestro Dylan senses that he adds to the fascination when he plays in the major, briefly slipping to minor in every fourth line – when the main character feels alone, when he gets hit by the heat of the night, when he feels empty inside, when he is despairing if she would ever pick him again.

Finally, a true bonanza is the arrangement. That was soon found, apparently: at the first recording session an acoustic version is already being tried and three days later, September 19th '74, at the second and last *Simple Twist* session, it is already final. Dylan's guitar and his literally lyrical vocals, Tony Brown on bass and a beautiful harmonica solo – *it is in working within limits that the master reveals himself*, as Goethe taught us.

The majority of followers trip over this decree, over those limits, the less-is-more commandment. Beautiful covers, no question about it – but that sacred trinity of singing, lyrics and music is lost in the sublime blues version of the mourned Sean Costello (with Levon Helm on drums, 2004), Jeff Tweedy's *Desire* approach, the chilling, majestic thriller of Concrete Blonde (*Still In Hollywood*, 1994), the dreamy, irresistible Jerry Garcia (live with the *Jerry Garcia Band*, 1991) ... it is a long line of great renditions that do not come close to the original.

The covers that do come close are sober. Diana Krall, for example. The very talented Mrs. Elvis Costello has distinguished herself previously in Dylanland - in 2015, for example, with missionary work for the ignored wallflower "Wallflower". She takes on *Simple Twist* alone, at the piano and equals the original's quantity of goose bumps with her enchanting singing art (2012). On a sympathetic little hobby project from Portland, the 4-song-EP *Buckets Of Rain* (2011), there is a fascinating, bone-dry version by the little-known St. Even to be found. A bit dressed up, granted (background vocals, occasional strumming on a scanty guitar, a stark piano), but this one time it works out quite well, partly thanks to the intimate living room sound of the recording.

Ah well, the song is practically indestructible... some lonesome lady with a guitar suffices, as Mrs. Stevie Ann shows in a Dutch TV show, in 2011.

3   You're A Big Girl Now

The *Men In Black* and a bunch of evil aliens are searching for 'The Light' of the planet Zartha, which eventually turns out to be a semi-divine creature in an attractive human form: Laura Vasquez, played by Rosario Dawson. That is tough luck for Agent Will Smith, who has an understandable crush on Laura. Laura, too, has a hard time saying goodbye, and instantly rain rustles down gently. Agent K, Tommy Lee Jones, knows why:

> "You are a Zarthan. When you get sad, it always seems to rain."
> "Lots of people get sad when it rains," Laura argues.
> K clarifies, pitying: "It rains *because* you're sad, baby."

Rain is an indestructible metaphor to the esteemed ladies and gentlemen poets. And as a rule, it symbolizes suffering and calamity; even in the Bible, where decors are generally arid, dry and destitute, rain usually means misery. The Lord drowns the whole world in forty days and nights of rain, lets fire, sulphur and hail-stones rain down, rains lash sassy Egyptians, it rains powder and dust upon idolaters, but paradoxically God thunders, when He is very, very angry, that He will *shut up heaven that there be no rain*.

The negative connotation penetrates world literature and of course also the work of the songwriters. It rains in the heart of Buddy Holly ("Raining In My Heart", 1959, written by the Bryant couple), the "Rain" of The Beatles causes people to flee, Sinatra's life is a cold rainy day after the departure of his sweetheart, ("Here's That Rainy Day") and the Gershwin brothers comfort and console that every dream home has its heartache ("Some Rain Must Fall", 1921).

It also rains in Dylan's catalogue. Dozens of times. In the early years, the poet usually brings it down to sharpen a dark, threatening and sometimes even gruesome content. The heavy rain in "A Hard Rain's A-Gonna Fall", of course, the body of Emmett Till is dragged to the river through a bloody, red rain, the Walls Of Red Wing are all the more despondent when the rain hits heavily on the roofs and filthy, pouring rain pierces Hollis Brown.

In the sixties, Dylan succumbs to the age-old, familiar connection of rain with heartbreak and related amorous misery. The protagonist from "Just Like A Woman" is in the rain, cats and dogs would come down *if not for you*, the converted Christian is left alone in the pouring rain by so-called friends ("I Believe In You"), or rolling through the rain when his lover has left him ("Dirt Road Blues").

The narrator in "You're A Big Girl Now" is back in the rain. That, plus the *little girl - big girl* mirroring, leads the listener involuntarily back to eight years earlier, to the I-figure from "Just Like A Woman", who is in the rain after yet another stranded love affair. Then, after Sad-Eyed Sara, the sun shines for the singer - up until *Blood On The Tracks*, the album on which Dylan is back in the rain and, by his own account, expresses *pain*.

Dylan confesses this shortly after the release of the album, in the radio interview with old friend Mary Travers (Peter, Paul and Mary), April 26, 1975: "A lot of people tell me they enjoy that album. It's hard for me to relate to that. I mean, you know, people enjoying the type of pain."

The statement is in line with son Jakob's famous quote in The New York Times, May 2010: "When I'm listening to 'Subterranean Homesick Blues', I'm grooving along just like you. But when I'm listening to 'Blood on the Tracks', that's about my parents."

Jakob's most quoted words, though meanwhile the nuance is lost that it is only an indirect quotation. It is true that it is printed in that interview with Jakob, but precisely this quote only appears in an intermezzo in which journalist DeCurtis recalls what Andrew Slater, the former manager of Jakob's band The Wallflowers, has told him about what Jakob supposedly said years earlier. It is hearsay, not words that the journalist has recorded from the mouth of Jakob Dylan.

Still, *pain*. The sharpest and most poignant that pain seems to be expressed in the final lines of "You're A Big Girl Now", in

> *I'm going out of my mind, oh, oh*
> *With a pain that stops and starts*
> *Like a corkscrew to my heart*
> *Ever since we've been apart*

The corkscrew metaphor is masterful. Only the harshest reviewer can hold back the tears here and the image resonates; it is a frequently cited verse line among biographers, reviewers and fans. In doing so, everyone follows Jakob's alleged observation and Dylan's own outpouring: the poet provides a rare, candid insight into the innermost workings of his soul, the man Bob Dylan reveals the pain he feels in losing his marital happiness, in losing Sara.

Sixteen years later, this openness is bothering him, and he tries to draw the curtain again. Dylan's tirade in the book accompanying the collection *Biograph* clashes head-on with Jakob's statement and Dylan's own commentary from 1975. Completely foolish is the thought that he would tell something from his own life. If you think so, you are nuts, he fulminates:

> "I read that this was supposed to be about my wife. I wish somebody would ask me first before they go ahead and print stuff like that. I mean, it couldn't be about anybody else but my wife, right? Stupid and misleading jerks these interpreters sometimes are ... I don't write confessional songs. Emotions got nothing to do with it. It only seems so, like it seems that Laurence Olivier is Hamlet... well, actually I did write one once and it wasnt very good - it was a mistake to record it and I regret it... back there somewhere on maybe my third or fourth album."

Dylan refers to the painful song "Ballad In Plain D", the vicious, nasty attack against Suze Rotolo and especially her sister Carla. This mea culpa at the end, however, hardly distracts from the main idea of this comment: suddenly the poet claims that he would never ever write about his own marriage - or about other private disputes.

For the *Biograph* box, Dylan opts for a New York recording, which is a chillingly beautiful version from September '74. Scantily instrumented, but with the tasteful, restrained organ by Paul Griffin, the virtuoso who so often manages to press the right key on Dylan recordings (the piano parts on "One Of Us Must Know" and "Like A Rolling Stone", for example) and with the steel guitar of Buddy Cage, the master of New Riders Of The Purple Sage. The sessions inspire Cage: the next New Riders album has a cover of "Farewell Angelina" (*Oh, What A Mighty Time*, produced by Bob Johnston).

When the recordings in New York have been completed and the album is ready to be pressed, Dylan goes to his family in Minnesota for Christmas. Brother David hears the pressings and has criticism which the maestro supports. The release is hastily postponed, and on 27 and 30 December 1974 Dylan re-records five of the ten songs with local musicians under the direction of David Zimmerman - including "You're A Big Girl Now".

The accompaniment on the Minneapolis version is less desolate, even opens with an elegant, almost sweet guitar mosaic, contrasting beautifully with Dylan's distraught recital - it is indeed difficult to choose between the two versions. Brother David may have stumbled over the uniformity of the ten tracks, not so much over the beauty of the individual tracks. Bootlegs like *Blood On The Outtakes* and *Blood On The Tapes,* and the official release *More Blood, More Tracks* feed that thought; ten songs in a row where the sound is predominantly dictated by Dylan's guitar and the bass of Tony Brown, does not detract from the otherwise undisputed splendour of the songs, but the impact of the album as a whole is affected (not to mention the incessant tickling of Dylan's cufflinks against his guitar).

The lyrics have a peculiar magic. The many acetous literators who, after the awarding the Nobel Prize, argue that a song is not literature because it cannot exist without the performance, are usually painfully ill-taught. Apart from the fact that one may also claim the same about the Nobel Prize-winning theatre writers: the majority of Dylan's lyrics are powerful enough to stimulate, touch or move even without the performance, easily survive on naked paper. But every now and then it does need the performance, like here, at "You're A Big Girl Now".

A few sparkling direct hits the lyrics certainly contain. The opening lines, for example, which immediately stimulate the listener and the reader;

> *Our conversation was short and sweet*
> *It nearly swept me off-a my feet*

These words promise the story of a man who has fallen madly in love. *To be swept off my feet* is the ecstatic variant to express *confusion* - in a positive, amorous sense. In the following lines, however, it suddenly becomes clear that the conversation was an exit conversation, that the narrator has been dumped and that he has lost the ground under his feet.

The aforementioned corkscrew metaphor is another literary bull's eye, but otherwise ... *on paper* the lyrics indeed do reek of melo-drama and overdone pathos, with clichéd exclamations like *I'm going out of mind* or *I can change, I swear*.

But then: the performance. Dylan the singer expresses a pain and a regret in his words, which also bestow an authenticity, truthful-ness and loneliness upon the less stimulating fragments - it may not be Nobel worthy literature, but Art with a capital A it certainly is.

The song has a beautiful melody, the notes are in the right place to enhance the dramatic, melancholy lyrical content, but still: that performance is decisive, as the many unsuccessful covers demonstrate. The astute quote from T.S. Eliot (*immature poets imitate, mature poets steal*) also applies to musicians. The artists who try to imitate Dylan's heartache (Lloyd Cole, My Morning Jacket, to name but two of the better-known) are whining, ruin a work of art. The colleagues who understand that they should not try to imitate Dylan, swing in the other direction, concentrate on the beauty of the composition and deliver a shiny, but flat, emotionless interpretation. Mary Lee's Corvette, for example (on her otherwise beautiful integral live performance of *Blood On The Tracks*, 2002), and even the grandmaster of the Dylan interpreters, the Texan Jimmy LaFave, is brilliant, but sterile (*Austin Skyline*, 1992).

The most enjoyable are the artists who only cherry pick the best bits, and stay far away from the pangs of love. The collective Zita Swoon from Antwerp (who already produced a attractive "Series Of Dreams") performs live a dreamy, hushed version which puts emphasis on the music, not on the lyrics. This is even more true for Dave's True Story, a jazz/pop band from New York that chooses a Steely Dan approach on their fascinating tribute project *Simple Twist Of Fate* (2005), an album with seven jazzy Dylancovers.

Only "It's All Over Now, Baby Blue" really does not fit in with the languid, nonchalant jazz arrangement, but the combo does produce, by far, the most beautiful cover of "You're A Big Girl Now". Two of them, even - the *radio edit* is slightly more compelling. Opening with a rustling cymbal – *I'm back in the rain.*

4   Idiot Wind

The song has since long been forgotten and covered in dust, when the teenager Ketch Secor first hears "Rock Me Mama (Like A Wagon Wheel)" in the 90s, the half-mumbled, unfinished patch of a non-existent song on *Peco's Blues* (1973) , a bootleg collection of session recordings from January and February 1973 for the soundtrack of *Pat Garrett And Billy The Kid*.

Teenagers, especially the male ones, are known to have a rather flexible prefrontal cortex, therefore they dare to ride down the hill in shopping carts, jump three floors down from the balcony into the hotel swimming pool and they do not mind messing around with a Dylan song. Ketch adds two great verses to the sketch, and merrily and often plays the song. Also he founded a band, the now world-famous Old Crow Medicine Show.

The boys record the song for a self-released EP (*Troubles Up And Down The Road*, 2001). In 2003 the band scores a record deal and, after copyright has been arranged with Dylan (it will be fifty-fifty), the song is recorded again, this time as the closing number for the

BLOOD ON THE TRACKS

acclaimed, untitled debut album from 2004. It is not a hit, it is not even released on single, but it is picked up. Initially by amateurs, on talent shows, by school bands, in karaoke bars and truck stops – the song is easy to play and has a high sing-along quality – but slowly and surely it seeps through to the higher echelons.

In 2013, Darius Rucker scores a number-1 hit with "Wagon Wheel" and the song finally penetrates the Great American Songbook. It yields Rucker a Grammy Award (Best Country Solo Performance, 2013) and membership of the Grand Ole Opry.

It does have a small spicy edge, Rucker's success. Before his solo career, Darius Carlos Rucker has been the face of Hootie & The Blowfish, the band with which he records five albums and sixteen hit singles, tours around the world and sells tens of millions of records (the debut album from 1994, *Cracked Rear Window*, achieves sixteen times platinum and is the 14th best-selling album of all time). One of the biggest successes is the world hit "Only Wanna Be With You" (1995) and that song leads to a conflict with Dylan. Rucker has plundered *Blood On The Tracks* a little too enthusiastically. Starting with a chip from "You're A Big Girl Now":

> *Put on a little Dylan*
> *Sitting on a fence*

Followed by a big bite from "Idiot Wind":

> *Said I shot a man named Gray*
> *Took his wife to Italy*
> *She inherited a million bucks*
> *And when she died it came to me*
> *I can't help it if I'm lucky*

And in case we still don't get it, the last verse opens with:

Yeah I'm tangled up in blue

Dylan's management of Dylan, the *thief of thoughts* who has a rather double-minded attitude with regard to citing someone else's work without acknowledging the source, mobilises lawyers, threatens with a copyright infringement indictment and eventually Hootie & The Blowfish settles the case, for an unknown, but undoubtedly substantial amount.

Anyhow, no hard feelings with Rucker, apparently. With "Wagon Wheel" he lines Dylan's pockets once again.

The lines quoted from the opening verse of "Idiot Wind" are the most enigmatic of one of Dylan's undisputed monuments. The remaining 574 words can be interpreted biographically without too much reading into it; if one song justifies the disqualification *Divorce Record*, it is this complex put-down. And therein, in the all too easily traceable private worries of the man Dylan, the puzzle's solution to that mysterious opening seems to lie.

In the interview with Robert Hilburn (September 2001), Dylan states:

> "I overwrite. If I know I am going in to record a song, I write more than I need. In the past that's been a problem because I failed to use discretion at times. I have to guard against that."

That concurs with the self-criticism he voiced in 1985, in the interview with Bill Flanagan for his book *Written In My Soul*:

Flanagan:

Have you ever put something in a song that was too personal? Ever had it come out and then said, "Hmm, gave away too much of myself there"?

Dylan:

I came pretty close with that song "Idiot Wind." That was a song I wanted to make as a painting. A lot of people thought that song, that album "Blood on the Tracks", pertained to me. Because it seemed to at the time. It didn't pertain to me. It was just a concept of putting in images that defy time - yesterday, today, and tomorrow. I wanted to make them all connect in some kind of a strange way. I've read that that album had to do with my divorce. Well, I didn't get divorced till four years after that. I thought I might have gone a little bit too far with "Idiot Wind." I might have changed some of it. I didn't really think I was giving away too much; I thought that it *seemed* so personal that people would think it was about so-and-so who was close to me. It wasn't. But you can put all these words together and that's where it falls. You can't help where it falls. I didn't feel that one was too personal, but I felt it *seemed* too personal. Which might be the same thing, I don't know. But it never was *painful*. 'Cause usually with those kinds of things, if you think you're too close to something, you're giving away too much of your feelings, well, your feelings are going to change a month later and you're going to look back and say, "What did I do that for?"

Flanagan:

But for all the power of "Idiot Wind," there's part of it that always cracked me up. You talk about being accused of shooting a man, running off with his wife, she inherits a million bucks, she dies, and the money goes to you. Then you say, "I can't help it if I'm lucky." (Laughter.)

Dylan:

Yeah, right. With that particular set-up in the front I thought I could say *anything* after that. If it did seem personal, I probably made it overly so - because I said too much in the front and still made it come out like, "Well, so what?"

Dylan once again asserts that he didn't think the song was too personal, didn't think he was giving away too much anywhere. And immediately afterwards, very Dylanesque, implies the opposite: "I mean, I give it all away, but I'm not giving away any secrets."

With that concluding remark, and with that laboriously meandering answer to Flanagan's question about indiscretion, Dylan again confirms the often quoted words from his son Jakob, in the *New York Times*, 10 May 2005: "When I listen to Blood On The Tracks, that's about my parents."

Also noteworthy is that Dylan mentions "Idiot Wind" when Flanagan asks if he is ever indiscrete. In the same year 1985, *Biograph* is released, the collection box with the rich liner notes recorded by Cameron Crowe. In it Dylan states - incidentally in response to "You're A Big Girl Now", another one of those allegedly indiscrete songs on *Blood On The Tracks* - that "Ballad In Plain D" is his only confessional song. And that he still regrets that one.

Autobiographical or not, "Idiot Wind" is a masterly, heart-breaking confessional song. If not from Dylan, then from a desperate archetype Disillusioned Love Partner.

The mastery lies within the vulnerability under the rawness. The narrator is mean, unreasonable and malicious, but does not succeed in becoming unsympathetic; we all hear the pain speaking, not the man himself. A corkscrew is twisted into his heart and just like a woman who curses her husband to hell during labour, this hurt, heartbroken man damns his beloved.

So the first verse is a diversionary manoeuvre, as Dylan himself explains. We see a witty echo fourteen years later, when Dylan, in line with the punch line *I can't help it if I'm lucky* calls himself *Lucky Wilbury* in The Traveling Wilburys.

A relationship with the following couplets of "Idiot Wind" there is not.

Self-pity colours the second verse, with pubertal indignation: *even you believe all that nonsense "they" tell about me*. Unbelievable! After all those years! The classic assertive defence, in short, of the husband who is confronted with adultery accusations. And like all adulterous spouses, this protagonist does not opt for a calm, credible denial, but for the unreasonable counterattack, trying to get into the victim role himself: how could you think that of me. My, what a bad person you are.

Only in the third and fourth verse does the poet of "Desolation Row", "She's Your Lover Now" and "Sign On The Cross" shine through again, the poet who, in the words of Joan Baez, is *so good at keeping things vague*. That third verse opens with other words than the original version from New York. Initially Dylan sings *I threw the I-Ching yesterday, it said there might be some thunder at the well*, a line the bard probably rewrites because it might seem too personal - in '65 he publicly, in an interview with the *Chicago Daily News*, stated:

"There is a book called the *I-Ching*, I'm not trying to push it, I don't want to talk about it, but it's the only thing that is amazingly true, period, not just for me. Anybody would know it. Anybody that ever walks would know it, it's a whole system of finding out things, based on all sorts of things. You don't have to believe in anything to read it, because besides being a great book to believe in, it's also very fantastic poetry."

The man Dylan apparently really has something with this *Book Of Changes*, so on closer inspection the poet prefers to omit a reference to it. Instead, he opts for the equally mystical, but somehow more run-of-the-mill *I ran into the fortune teller, who said beware of lightning that might strike*. In terms of content, no major difference, of course: both variants describe a supernatural entity warning of a fatal, major event. And not too far from the person behind the poet, by the way; from his autobiography *Chronicles* we can conclude that Dylan is not completely insensitive to the transcendent. Concepts such as *fate*, *destiny* and *spiritual* come along dozens of times, even when he documents something as everyday as a break-up (in this case with Suze Rotolo): "*Eventually fate flagged it down and it came to a full stop*."

Evoked images and chosen language in the continuation of this occult opening line seem familiar. A lonely soldier on the cross, a chestnut mare, the accumulation of antitheses (*peace / war, truth / lies, he won after losin', woke up / daydreamin*) ... familiar Dylan territory. The image of the smoke-emitting freight car (*smoke pourin' out of a boxcar door*) is such an image that could have surfaced in "A Hard Rain's A-Gonna Fall" or "Farewell, Angelina". Impenetrable, but a strong stage piece, a piece scenery for a painting by Dalí or a twentieth-century Hieronymous Bosch - Dylan now and then succeeds in his intention to make the songs on *Blood On The Tracks* "like a painting". That probably also explains the textual intervention with this excerpt. Originally *watchin' falling raindrops pour*; from a radically different perspective, and visually much less strong than that smoldering wagon.

Bitter revenge, however, colours the last, lurid lines, in which the narrator accuses his beloved of hurtful lies and daydreams about her fate: her corpse in a ditch, flies buzzing around her dead eyes and her blood dripping along the saddle of that chestnut mare. A macabre, cinematic image that the thief of thoughts with a sense of tradition borrows from a nineteenth-century cowboy ballad, from "There's Blood On The Saddle," recorded in 1937 by the renowned Alan Lomax for the Library Of Congress.

This structure the poet extends in the fifth and sixth verse. Again a mystical opening ("destiny broke us apart"), a series of contradictions (*good / bad, upside down, top / bottom, spring / autumn, I waited on the running boards*), another hint to the yin yang of the I-Ching (*the good is bad and the bad is good*) and highly visual, wild metaphors. "You tamed the lion in my cage" can be placed, but what about "The priest wore black on the seventh day"? One might hear an echo of "Highway 61 Revisited" and as a character he fits effortlessly on *Blonde On Blonde*, but what bussiness does that priest have here? And why is the storyteller waiting on the running boards, at the cypresses?

The poet achieves at least the same as in the third verse: the setting in which his lying, blinded and shameful beloved is residing, is a filled tableau, perhaps in California, the land without seasons, and otherwise in an expressionistic representation of a Promised Land – it is, after all, both spring and fall in these parts, *time is defied*.

The real pain, bitterness and despair the poet saves for the last verses. The opening lines of the seventh verse are the most abrasive of the entire song. The narrator here exposes himself to such an extent that the listener gets the uncomfortable feeling of unwittingly reading someone else's diary: he no longer tolerates her touch, not even indirectly, sneaks past her closed door ... this is getting too painful. In that furious live version from '76 (*Hard Rain*), Dylan puts it even more lachrymosely: "I can't even touch the clothes you wear, very time I come into your door, you leave me standing in the middle of the air."

In the earlier version, from September, the poet opens this seventh verse less whiny. There he even expresses a shared guilt: *We pushed each other a little too far*, and he describes the inconvenience of the silent treatment ("In order to get in a word with you, I'd have had to come up with some excuse").

Three months later, in Minnesota, the poet deletes those resigned lines and reignites the vindictive slander again. Awkward is the hurtful, childish self-pity with which the narrator tries to throw the final jabs, hooks and punches ("You'll never know the hurt I suffered") and the ridiculous, misplaced, acted superiority of the punchline *it makes me feel so sorry*.

Multicoloured and complex enough, those eight verses, but the status and reputation of the song are coined by the false, cutting chorus, in which the disillusioned narrator *ad nauseam* argues what an imbecile his ex-lover is. Of mythical proportions, is her silliness. When she starts speaking, the IQ drops from the Grand Coulee Dam (in the state of Washington, in the far west) to the Capitol (in Washington, D.C., in the far east), so throughout the country. The backwardness of her words stirs up dust, fluttering curtains, blows through our coats and desecrates the letters we wrote. The chorus is, in short, a put-down that even surpasses "Like A Rolling Stone", "Positively 4th Street" and "She's Your Lover Now" in malice. That false personality shift from the last chorus ("*We're* idiots, babe") does not alleviate it.

The intensity of Dylan's rendering ("black energy and poison," as band member David Mansfield calls it) during the *Rolling Thunder Revue*, the 1976 concert tour, makes it difficult to ignore personal, intimate involvement with the words sung. Here is really an artist who exposes the person behind the artist. Tension releasing, presumably, and after 1976 the bard seems to be relieved; "Idiot Wind" disappears from the set list. In the following years, however, the song remains a topic of discussion in interviews, sometimes at the initiative of Dylan himself, as in the above conversation with Flanagan in 1985. Or in 1987, when the director of the "multi-media musical" *Dylan: Words & Music*, Peter Landecker, says that he has spoken with Dylan:

> "We talked about the show, which songs are included and why. Dylan asked if *Idiot Wind* was in. I said no and asked why he singled out that one. "It's one of the most theatrical, dramatic ones", he said."

And in '91, in the interview with Paul Zollo for *SongTalk*, Dylan goes into the work in more detail. It even seduces him into an atypical expression of pride. Regarding the different text versions of "Idiot Wind", the poet states: "There could be a myriad of versions for the thing. It doesn't stop. It wouldn't stop. Where do you end?"

Dylan then pays some attention to people's reactions to his songs and concludes his answer to Zollo's question about "Idiot Wind" with a modest, yet satisfied, qualification:

> "There's just something about my lyrics that just have a gallantry to them. And that might be all they have going for them. [*Laughs*]. However, it's no small thing."

That *is* intriguing. Of all songs, Dylan chooses "Idiot Wind", one of the most nasty and indiscrete songs in his oeuvre, to articulate a comprehensive qualification of his lyrics: they have a *gallantry*. That, as we can expect from Dylan, is by no means a unambiguous valuation. "Gallantry" can mean *courage*, *fearlessness*, as well as *elegance*, *nobility*, *courtesy*. The rest of the interview, Dylan is pretty clear, informative and serious, so we can assume that he is not throwing one of his good old smokescreens here, but that he means what he says.

In that case we can delete the meaning *courtesy*; Dylan himself also acknowledges that battery acid is the fuel of this song and would agree it is not really courteous, well-mannered to sing someone's poor mental capacities for almost eight minutes.

Then remains: *courageous*, *brave*, *fearless*, "gallantry" as the opposite of cowardice. There is something to be said for that. At least: with this specific song. The narrator is not afraid to expose himself, that much is true. Whether, and to what extent, the qualification also applies to Dylan's catalog at all is another question. Among the majority of the Dylan followers, the word *courageous* will not come up to characterize the man's work.

At public praises such as the Oscar ceremony or the Nobel Prize enough adjectives are listed to praise Dylan's work, but practically nothing that comes close to *bravery*. In fact, Dylan is pretty much the only one who repeatedly points out the *gallantry* of his work.

Here, in this conversation with Zollo, as he also does in the (not too serious) interview with Jonathan Cott for Rolling Stone in 1977, alleging that the driving force behind *Blood On The Tracks* in general and "Idiot Wind" in particular is *willpower*. And again, for example, in his reaction to winning an Oscar for "Things Have Changed":

> "I want to thank the members of the Academy who were bold enough to give me this award for this song, which obviously… a song that doesn't pussyfoot around nor turn a blind eye to human nature."

Lofty words, but it is highly questionable whether the jury members recognize their choice in Dylan's words. "Things Have Changed" is a beautiful, Oscar-worthy song, but a song which *doesn't pussyfoot around*? The lyrics are full of disguising language ("some things", "so much", "things have changed", "lot of other stuff" and so on) and dark imagery. "I've been walking forty miles of bad road" (Dylan writes in the fortieth year after his first record). A feeling comes over him as if he wants to put a worshiped lady in a wheelbarrow (?). The "next sixty seconds could be like an eternity" (the singer sings exactly sixty seconds before the end of the song). And the ultimate enigmatic verse of the last middle-eight, about one Mr. Jinx and Miss Lucy who jumped into a lake.

All in all, Dylan clearly has a different definition of *gallantry*, of boldness or courage, than the average jury member or the average Dylan follower.

All that talk about "Idiot Wind" leads to an unexpected, short revival: 1992, we are in Australia and suddenly "Idiot Wind" is on the setlist again. In Melbourne, April 5, he announces the song with the surprising words "Thank you, that was a recent song," but presumably Dylan means the song he played before (1990's "Cat's In The Well"). In California, a few weeks later, he calls it an *old song*. He does not comment further on the unexpected choice, or on the song at all.

They are beautiful performances. The singer mainly follows the *Blood On The Tracks* version, the lyrics are not completely accurate and two couplets are dropped in favour of a harmonica solo. Nothing is left of the fury of sixteen years earlier (obviously), but more love has been given to the musical accompaniment - an ebb and flow arrangement with a spotlight on the steel guitar, giving the song an attractive country atmosphere.

Dylan plays it forty times, that spring and summer of '92, and then brings the song "home"; the performance in Minneapolis, 30 August, is the very last one.

The colleagues stay far away from "Idiot Wind", although the song is usually somewhere in the top 20 in the various lists of Best Dylan Songs. It is understandable, this restraint; too personal, despite everything the master undertook to make it only *seem* personal.

Mary Lee's Corvette of course cannot avoid the song, when (magnificently) performing an integral *Blood On The Tracks: Recorded Live At Arlene's Grocery* (2001), but with "Idiot Wind" singer Mary Lee Kortes loses track sometimes. The band makes up for a lot.

Safer, because instrumental, is jazz guitarist Jef Lee Johnson, who passed away too early, on his beautiful tribute album *The Zimmerman Shadow* (2009), a record with bold, mostly successful interpretations of sometimes exotic, exurbantly fanning out Dylan songs ("As I Went Out One Morning" develops into an exciting , fierce Jimi Hendrix-like 11-minute jazz exercise, for example). Johnson's "Idiot Wind" remains serene and is supported by a tasteful, funky bass part, over which Johnson plays a partly pointy, partly dreamy guitar part - very attractive.

The only other notable professional cover is from The Coal Porters, the British-American bluegrass band of the respectable Dylanologist Sid Griffin, author of two excellent Dylan books. The first album, *How Dark This Earth Will Shine* (2004) is very nice, the bluegrass version of the old punk hit "Teenage Kicks" (The Undertones, 1978) is great, but "Idiot Wind" is a less fortunate choice; the veranda atmosphere does not really fit the song.

The amateurs are as enthusiastic as the pros are reluctant. YouTube is teeming with, mostly pathetic, living room recordings, though the diversity is striking. Lots of spectacled, white males in their fifties, of course, but also surprisingly many younger hipsters, blushing, shy teenagers and even some local heroes with homemade translations (Swedish and Hebrew, for example). Artistically not too uplifting, but it does reflect the indestructible appeal of the song over the decades.

The Old Crow Medicine Show has not risked it either. The band received a lot of applause in 2016 with the tribute *50 Years Of Blonde On Blonde*, the live registration of a complete rework of that legendary album. The accompanying tour, which leads the men to Europe as well, is just as successful, their "Wagon Wheel" was awarded an official Seal Of Approval from the master himself, as well as the successor "Sweet Amarillo" (at Dylan's request completed by Ketch Secor and his men), so in 2025, at the fiftieth anniversary of *Blood On The Tracks*, we can expect the next recommendable cover of "Idiot Wind".

5   You're Gonna Make Me Lonesome When You Go

"There's a code in the lyrics," Dylan says in 1978 about *Blood On The Tracks* in the interview with Jonathan Cott. The odd duck out among those encrypted, coded texts that supposedly dominate the album is "You're Gonna Make Me Lonesome When You Go". Thematically (Love & Loss) the song remains in the tracks, but despite the title the song is not about loss, farewell or pain. It does express bittersweet melancholy, but an enamoured cheerfulness prevails. That focus is primarily due to the musical accompaniment, of course - especially thanks to the tempo and the harmonica Dylan elevates the song to jittery joy. And secondly to the reason: the poet *is* in love.

Equally different is the relative unequivocalness. Dylan usually denies the more coherent interpretations, especially the biographical ones. Therein he goes quite far.

"Sara" is not necessarily about Sara, he states with a straight face in the same interview. For this song such a denial would be at least as absurd. Ellen Bernstein, no doubt.

In 1974, the married Dylan has a rather open, short love affair with the 24-year-old Ellen Bernstein, an employee at Columbia Records. When she hears this list of place names, she is probably the first listener in the world to realize that "You're Gonna Make Me Lonesome When You Go" is about her. *I'll look for you in old Honolulu, San Francisco, Ashtabula* ... Ellen was born in Ashtabula and then lived in Honolulu and San Francisco. And she also knows where the Queen Anne's lace reference comes from. Ellen stays with Dylan at his farm in Minnesota and during a walk through the purple clover (*trifolium pratense*) she reveals that all too majestic name for wild carrot (*daucus carota*).

Not only the name, but also the myths surrounding and etymology of Queen Anne's Lace, probably charm the bard. The safest assumption is that the predilection for lace of the English Queen Anne (1665-1714) led to the naming; the network of the many, delicate little flowers does indeed look a bit like lace. By the way, Anne was the wife of King James I, the king to whom we owe the famous Bible translation KJV, *King James Version*, which is open on a stand in the middle of Dylan's study.

More romantic is the theory that the name refers to Anne Boleyn, who was beheaded by order of King Henry VIII in 1536, wearing a lace collar. The purple-pink floral heart in the middle, surrounded by that 'lace', represents Boleyn's decapitated neck, is the idea. And the botanical works never omit the warning that we must watch out for the poisonous twin sister of this wild carrot, for *conium maculatum*: poison hemlock, the poison that Socrates took after he was sentenced to death for wickedness - again one of those fun facts that will appeal to an obfuscater and masquerade fan like Dylan.

Apart from the music, the pastoral landscape descriptions, the melancholy and the absence of bitter cynicism and/or dylanesque scorn ensure a sunny *couleur locale*. The relationship is already over, but the narrator still feels a fond afterglow. Very different, apparently, this affair. Previous love relationships were all like "Verlaine and Rimbaud", so relationships with extreme highs and lows, with devastating love and bloody hatred - but this amourette is by no means comparable, "there's no way I can compare all those scenes to this affair".

That is a sweet little lie; to the moonlight and roses of those earlier loves, this summer with Bernstein is perfectly comparable. The decor for example. In Dylan's rare (past) love lyric without viciousness, bitter words and cynicism, we are invariably in an idyllic countryside. That earlier *Girl from the North Country* (Bernstein is also a North Country Girl, Ashtabula is located on Lake Erie, on the opposite bank is Canada) was idealized in a radiant, crisp snowy landscape, with "Tough Mama" Dylan is tumbling in a flower meadow, the adored in "New Morning" is sung between frisking bunnies and woodchucks, babbling brooks in the summer sun. Long hair every immaculate loved one also has, and flowers usually adorn the idyll.

The same goes for Dylan's continual preoccupation with *time*. It is a constant in his work anyway, and also in his love lyric the narrator always refers to the distorting effect love has on his sense of time. In "Boots Of Spanish Leather" he wants his time to be *more easy passin'*, *Ramona* captures the minutes with her magnetic movements, "time" is the ultimate sacrifice he promises his beloved in "Pledging My Time", without her, life is a eternal winter ("If Not For You"), time passes slowly when you're searching for love ("Time Passes Slowly") and passes so quickly when she is with you ("New Morning"), and also here, in "You're Gonna Make Me Lonesome When You Go" her absence at first has a delaying effect (*so slow*) and later, when she is there, she makes him forget the time (*never realize the time*). Very similar, in short, with all those earlier love stories of the narrator.

On one level, however, it is indeed different from all those other occassions: on an orthographic level. This is the only song in which Dylan, also in the official *Lyrics*, spells the word combination *you're* as *yer*. Not in the title, remarkably enough, otherwise consistent. Only in the poem *Last Thoughts On Woody Guthrie* (1963) Dylan also writes *yer*, but as a spelling of *your* (and also inconsistently) - *you're* is spelled correctly. Of course, Dylan usually sings "yer", in order to rhyme with *her* (like in "I Wanna Be Your Lover": *I don't wanna be hers, I wanna be yours*) and in manuscripts and typoscripts we sometimes see "y'r" or other variants, but in the official publications, in the song collections and on the website, it is always proper and civilized *you're* and *your*. It is a thing, for a moment, when a good-natured, ironic Lennon sings his "Yer Blues" on *White Album* (1968), with that famous Dylan reference (*I feel so suicidal, just like Dylan's Mr. Jones*), but that does not move Dylan to spelling phonologically either.

This one time it is probably an insider's wink to Miss Bernstein. After all, she also is from that corner of the United States and *yer* is typical of the dialect over there. Just like *furget it*, *furever*, *git* and *gitting* (from "to get") and *hunnert* ("hundred").

Alright then, in this one single sub-area, on an orthographic level, this affair is unique, incomparable with all those earlier Verlaine-and-Rimbaud-like relations.

The version recorded in New York in September '74 belongs to the five songs that have endured the critical ears of Dylan himself and his brother David, so it does not have to be re-recorded in Minneapolis, in December. Maybe that's a pity. Presumably, a re-recording would have been more melancholy, slower and frugal. That alternative is to be found in many covers. "You're Gonna Make Me Lonesome" is picked up by a lot of colleagues and roughly we see a dichotomy: one half follows the music and delivers a danceable up-tempo country version; the other half is guided by the lyrics and produces a slightly sad pop ballade.

The country faction includes a surprising Miley Cyrus, who in 2012, shortly before her downfall, radiates on Amnesty's *Chimes Of Freedom*. That version inspires half a generation of female country artists (Danielle Lowe, Emily Morgan), who no longer surprise. However, they are all indebted to the superior Shawn Colvin (1994, *Cover Girl*).

Hints of such a fictional, missed Minneapolis recording can be found with a touching Mary Lou Lord (2000) and devout Dylan tributers Andy Hill & Renee Safier (on *It Takes A Lot To Laugh*, 2001), but the most beautiful tear jerker is from the incidental duo Tom Corwin & Tim Hockenberry (on *Mostly Dylan*, 2005), including a guitar that gently weeps.

A fascinating hybrid of these two varieties comes from Romania. Translated, unfortunately ("Ma Lasi Prea Singur Daca Vei Pleca", 1999), Alexandru Andries beautifully blends an upbeat country-like shuffle with Slavic melancholy.

Hors concours, finally, the enchanting Madeleine Peyroux, jazzy, cool and sexy, shines on *Careless Love*, 2004. There is no way to compare all those covers to this affair.

The Blood brother of Villon

When *Blood On The Tracks* is finally in stores, January 1975, on the back of the cover is a fierce, expressive and intriguing essay by celebrated journalist and author Pete Hamill from New York. Hamill travels and works all over the world, is there in Vietnam, Nicaragua and Northern Ireland, lives in Europe for years, is one of the four men who in 1968 overpower the murderer of Bobby Kennedy, Sirhan Sirhan, and publishes in the premier league, in magazines such as *The New Yorker, the Saturday Evening Post, Esquire, Playboy* and *Rolling Stone*.

Already in November '74 *Rolling Stone* dedicates an article to *Blood On The Tracks*. It is written by the well-informed Larry Sloman, who, like the rest of the world, including Dylan, still believes the album will be released in the next few days. He knows the September recordings from New York, has even seen the provisional cover ("a photo of a huge red rose against a white background") and knows that Dylan is looking for "old photos of his performance in Gerde's Folk City", meant for the back cover.

Sloman has spoken with the directly involved Dylan explorer John Hammond and with session musicians such as Barry Kornfeld, Eric Weissberg, Charlie Brown and Buddy Cage. And with colleague Pete Hamill, who briefly puts the essence of his essay into words, in a somewhat less elegant idiom, than one might perhaps wish for. A little more than two hundred words, of which two times *fucking*, once *fuck*, once *bitch* and once *cunt*, to express his admiration for the album, culminating in the conclusion: "the album is just fucking wonderful."

The Hamill fragment is introduced with the notion that Dylan has personally asked Hamill to write the liner notes. In an interview with the *Irish Times*, June 4, 2011 ("Bright Lights, Big City," written by Hamill's long-term friend George Kimball), the Grammy winner confirms:

> In 1962 I wrote a series about 42nd Street called *Welcome to Lostville*. One result was that the young Bob Dylan read it and invited me to his first concert at Town Hall; the result was a kind of friendship that years later led to my liner notes for *Blood on the Tracks*.

Dylan, whom he apparently regards as "a kind of friend", has not yet had his advancing insight into Minneapolis in the fall of '74, so when Hamill gets to work, he bases his essay on the New York recordings of the songs - hence the small "errors" in the cited song fragments.

For the second pressing, Hamill's contribution is removed and replaced by a cover-size image of an artwork by David Oppenheim. Also nice, but when Hamill receives a Grammy Award for *Best Album Notes* on 28 February 1976, CBS recognizes that painting over the essay might not have been a good move. From the third pressing on, the original liner notes are restored to their former glory.

Perhaps a touch too purple and a bit too pathetic here and there, but Hamill does know how to articulate very clearly and transparently the exceptional beauty of the album: in the space that Dylan leaves open, the space into which the listener is sucked.

Why the essay is removed in the second pressing is unclear. Most Dylanologists ignore this unusual manoeuvre and some suggest it was *for various reasons*, so they don't know either. But Robert Shelton (*No Direction Home*) reports that Dylan himself has cut it ("He scrapped an elegiac liner-note essay by Pete Hamill") and Shelton is usually well informed, of course.

The most likely scenario therefore is that Dylan has felt uncomfortable with the *himmelhochjauchzende*, the over-the-moon words of Hamill's essay, and considers the excess as self-glorification, that he experiences the liner notes as vain and overbearing. Writing something nice about him is not off limits, as for example Johnny Cash does on *Nashville Skyline* ("he is a hell of a poet"), but Hamill's essay does indeed come close to a canonization, to the embarrassing *voice-of-a-generation* appointments.

Pete Hamill, however, is still proud of his award-winning essay, shows it off on his website, it is mentioned in almost every article about Hamill and his publisher also recognizes its promotional power and invariably reports it with every new book presentation.

And right they are.

6   Meet Me In The Morning

They are bad to the bone, the Three Witches in Shakespeare's *Macbeth*. In the opening scene they forge their conspiracy, in the course of the drama they turn Macbeth's head, make misleading predictions and summon treacherous spirits. But they themselves can also crawl and tremble: when their supreme boss Hecate, the goddess of witchcraft, crossroads, poison plants and related misery, learns that the ladies on their own bring calamity, she furiously calls them to account. *"Meet me in the morning,"* she thunders, "in Hell, by the River of Woe, at the pit of Acheron."

Although the *honey* in Dylan's song does not have to go to Hell, she must also report at dawn, at the at least equally difficult to reach intersection "56th and Wabasha". In Dylan's birth state Minnesota there is indeed a Wabasha, and Wabasha Streets can also be found (in St. Paul, for example), but a crossing with a 56th does not exist. The poet chooses this combination only because of the pleasant consonance of these syllables, that is clear. The intended destination is not a bait - taking the adored one to a wet and cold Kansas is not exactly the promise of a Shangri-La. The protagonist waits therefore in vain, lonely and alone in the next verse, in that darkest hour just before sunrise.

The dawn is announced by a desolate crowing rooster in the distance, apparently feeling as miserable as the narrator. A verse later the birds fly low - it is going to rain, too. No matches in his pocket and the station is still closed; neither heat nor shelter for our tragic hero, here at that abandoned intersection of Wabasha and 56th. He is still there at sunset. No deprivation, hailstorm, nor hound dogs who chase him through the barbed wire, depress him deeper than this desolation, the desolation that makes his heart sink in his shoes.

At first glance a conventional *My Baby Left Me* blues theme, but it is certainly not a conventional blues text. The form is classical enough. Repeating the first verse line is common in the blues, as is the rhyme scheme, but everything else is unconventional, or at least unusual in the blues canon and in music at all.

Embedded is the story of the unhappy lover in a "round" frame. The lament starts at sunrise and ends at sunset. Dylan borrows this perhaps from Rimbaud, who, in his *Illuminations* (XVI and XXXIV, for example) and in various poems, frames his exurbant poetry tightly between dawn and dusk (or vice versa). And Rimbaud did not invent that, of course. William Blake loves the day/night structure, Goethe regularly uses it (*Willkommen und Abschied*, for example) and well, already in Sophocles' *Oedipus* the Sphinx means "a whole life" with her famous riddle that runs from morning till night.

Within this framework, Dylan interlaces the lyrical painting of man's suffering with his characteristic poetry of, as expressed by the secretary of the Nobel Prize committee, sampled tradition and pictorial thinking. *The darkest hour before dawn* from the second verse, for example, is perhaps a tribute to Clarence "Gatemouth" Brown's "Just Before Dawn", Zappa's all-time favourite guitar player. Dylan is also a fan; he puts Gatemouth three times on the playlist of his radio show. More likely, however, Dylan's reverence is meant for Ralph Stanley of The Stanley Brothers, who come in no less than five times in *Theme Time Radio Hour*. The Stanley brothers experienced a brief renaissance after Ralph's beautiful a-capella version of the classic "O, Death" in the Coen film *O Brother, Where Art Thou* (2000). It even earned him a Grammy.

Dylan has known the Stanleys much longer and certainly also their gospel classic "The Darkest Hour Is Just Before Dawn":

The sun is slowly sinkin'
The day's almost gone
Still darkness falls around us
And we must journey on

The darkest hour is just before dawn
The narrow way leads home
Lay down your soul at Jesus' feet
The darkest hour is just before dawn

The song resonates. Not only because of that deep dark hour before dawn - the opening line echoes into the closing sequence of "Meet Me In The Morning", the biblical *narrow way* later inspires a whole song on *Tempest* (2012).

Dylan produces, in short, sparkling antique poetry in a song text that is much more than a run-of-the-mill blues lamento.

In a sense, this also applies to the musical accompaniment. An ordinary blues scheme pressed into a similarly trivial blues stub, yet Dylan, or rather: the band, lifts it above a common blues. That band is led by maestro Eric Weissberg, who has scored a world hit a year and a half before this with the soundtrack for the film *Deliverance* (1972). A rightly acclaimed thriller with star actors Burt Reynolds and Jon Voight on a career peak, about four city friends who during a weekend trip through nature get into conflict with backward, inbred hillbillies.

The film causes a stir with a controversial male rape scene, but the most memorable scene is *Dueling Banjos*, the scene in which, after a hesitant start, one of the citymen with his guitar loses a splashing musical duel to a retarded, but virtuoso banjo playing peasant boy. The rest of the soundtrack is also provided by Weissberg plus companions and is just as attractive as the hit.

The folky bluegrass atmosphere the men bring with them to New York, when invited to record *Blood On The Tracks*. Here, in this song, it proves to be a golden combination, almost as fortunate as it was with the Nashville Cats at *Blonde On Blonde*. With Weissberg and his followers the potentially sharp, urban blues is transferred to the veranda, to the veranda of J.J. Cale to be precise.

A special star role is for steel guitarist Buddy Cage, who plays the solo on the last verse. It is an overdub, and the story behind the recording has become almost mythical. That story is recorded by Andy Gill and Kevin Odegard in *A Simple Twist or Fate: Bob Dylan and the Making of Blood on the Tracks* (2004).

Buddy Cage is by no means a minor player, he replaces Jerry Garcia in the New Riders Of The Purple Sage for example, but he does not have it easy, that September evening in 1974:

> "Let me do it two or three times, and you'll have it - I'm that quick - and he can plug them in wherever he wants, the choices would be up to him and Bob. But that's not what Dylan wanted, apparently: He ended up flashing the light time after time after time, and I found myself having to do six or seven takes."
> Worse still, there was little guidance as to what was wrong with the interrupted takes.
> "Not only was my wrist getting tired, but there was no conversation, no instructions, no nothing," Cage recalls, "just `Do it again, do it again.' I was getting really uncomfortable. Then finally the door to the control room opened, and Dylan comes striding out, walks straight up to my steel, and sticks the toes of his cowboy boots under my pedal bar. I don't know why he did that -- maybe for emphasis. Anyway, he does that and says, 'The first five verses is singin' -- you don't play; the last verse is playin' -- you play!' plunks his toes out from under my pedal steel bar, turns, and strides back into the control room."

Behind the glass window it is getting pretty crowded, Cage tells. Producer Phil Ramone, Dylan, Mick Jagger happens to be there, John Hammond and another five or six curious people. Cage feels humiliated, but recovers:

> "I thought, *well, you little fuck, I'm taller than you, and you're not gonna get away with that!* Phil came on the phones then - he was clearly uncomfortable too - and he said, *You wanna practice one?* and I said, *No - print it!* So the red light came on and I just did one take."

Cage plays lightly over the sung verses and then nails the searing break through the song's closing stages. He knows he nailed it, does not feel like a further humiliation or intervention, does not even wait for the track to finish, but abruptly walks away, striding into the control room. The first one he sees there is Dylan.

> "When I busted into the control room, he was laughin' his a** off! I looked at Ramone, and he was shakin' his head, sayin', *that was beautiful!* John Hammond said, *man, that was unbelievable!* I just looked at Dylan and said, **** *you!* and he just laughed -- he said, *well, we got it!*"

It was a performance by Dylan, designed to bring the best out of Cage.

> "He felt that was the way to get to me, and he broke the ice," says Cage, who instantly realized what Dylan had done. "It was wonderful! I was really grateful."

The colleagues agree. Steve Elliot opts for a melancholic, folky interpretation (on the beautiful tribute project *May Your Song Always Be Sung*, 2003), soberly set with two acoustic guitars. Much more violence produces the opulently hairstyled guitarist Jason Becker, who excels in virtuoso heavy metal - until tragedy strikes; in 1990 the terrible disease ALS is diagnosed. A few years later Becker cannot talk anymore and he cannot move anything except his eyes, but he remains musically active. His "Meet Me In The Morning" is, by his standards, a rather quiet version, to be found on the otherwise instrumental LP *Perspective* (1996), the first ever record of an ALS patient.

Melancholy and compelling is the blood-curdling live version by David Gray. The song is often on his set list in 2009 and 2010, the recording of March 29, 2010 from the Center For The Arts in Eagle Rock is one of the finest.

The many other covers - Black Crows, Carolyn Wonderland, Texas Diesel, Sloan Wainwright, just to name a few - are all beautiful, or at least pleasant. Remarkably enough, Sinéad O'Connor, who seldom misses the mark at a Dylan cover, sings one of the less successful versions (2012). Fantastic harmonica accompaniment, though.

Most of all, however, Dylan himself will be struck by the cover from a legendary blues hero: Freddie King on his last album, *Larger Than Life* from 1975, and, even more powerful and more frenzied, the version on the posthumously released live-album *Texas Flyer* (2010), recorded shortly before his death. That recognition may have touched the Bard even more than a Nobel Prize.

7   Lily, Rosemary And The Jack Of Hearts

It is not really Joan Baez' forte, writing songs, but at least once she rises above herself: "Diamonds & Rust" from 1975 really is a wonderful song. Definitely on a musical level, although the beauty may be due more to the sparkling arrangement than to the strength of the composition, but remarkably successful this one time are the lyrics and especially their tone. The lyrics of Baez are usually somewhat too larmoyant or one-dimensional and humourless ("To Bobby", for example), lyrics that are, in Dylan's words, "lousy poetry". "Diamonds & Rust" is pleasantly mild-mocking, honestly poignant, melancholic and poetic, a song in which Baez looks back, without any bitterness, at her time with Dylan, at that time they lived together in that crummy hotel over Washington Square (Hotel Earle on MacDougal Street and Wavery Place, a four-minute walk from 161 West Fourth Street, incidentally) and she remains on the right side of sentimentality from start to finish.

Equally remarkable is the origin story. That story the singer tells in the song itself: out of nowhere Dylan reports by phone, from a booth in the Midwest (on February 4, 1974 Dylan is with The Band in Denver - that would be an educated guess) and in 2010, in the *Huffington Post*, she adds another detail. "He read me the entire lyrics of *Lily, Rosemary and the Jack of Hearts*, that he'd just finished."

It inspires her to totally re-work the song she was just working on and to change it to "Diamonds & Rust"; "It had nothing to do with what it ended up as."

The inspiration comes, obviously, first and foremost from the unexpected conversation itself. But secondly perhaps also from the constellation of the acting persons in Dylan's song: two attractive women and an inscrutable, mysterious stranger - it is only a small bridge to the triangle Sara (or Suze), Joan and Dylan. For the costuming of those persons, Dylan then apparently looks at his pack of tarot cards, from which he seems to draw more often in the 1970s. His mysterious hint from 1977, in the interview with Jonathan Cott, who tries to push him into all sorts of tarot symbolism, seems a vague confirmation: *there's a code in the lyrics*, meaning the song lyrics of *Blood On The Tracks*. The continuation of that outpouring ("there's no sense of time") is comprehensible, but that code has not been cracked yet - if there is one, of course.

Dylan, in any case, inhibits the over-enthusiastic reach for *The Pictorial Key to the Tarot* (A.E. Waite, 1910). "I'm not really too acquainted with that, you know," he says a half year later to the same Cott in a follow-up interview, when the journalist starts to blabber about all the tarot symbolism he has discovered in Dylan's lyrics. And a few years later, in an interview with music journalist Neil Spencer, he repeats that evasion almost verbatim: "I didn't get into the Tarot Cards all that deeply."

Undoubtedly some echoes will have trickled down, that much is true. The names for example. The *lily* and the *rose* are the only flowers at the feet of The Magician, "the divine Apollo, smiling with confidence, with radiant eyes", the tarot figure in whom Robert Shelton too thinks seeing traits from Bob Dylan (*Melody Maker*, July 29 1978) and to whom more references can be found (on *Street Legal*, in particular). And once in that tarot tunnel, references are to be found in each of the sixteen couplets. But in the end, all those references are probably in the category that Dylan is referring to in his Nobel speech: "I've written all kinds of things into my songs. And I'm not going to worry about it – what it all means."

Sobering words, in line with earlier relativizations with which Dylan dismisses the all too exuberant and pompous exegesis of his lyrics. Above all, It has to *sound* good, he says in the same speech - I have been influenced like everyone else, and it can mean anything

This also applies to the symbols in this song. The lily and the rose, Lily and Rosemary, is one of those combinations that we can already find in the Bible, in the Song of Songs (2:1, "I am the rose of Sharon, and the lily of the valleys"), a Bible book that is probably deeper under Dylan's skin than those tarot cards.

In terms of content, the story is not easy to follow. The plot looks classic enough; on the surface it is a weekday cowboy novel with all the clichés involved. A mysterious stranger, a bank robbery, there is poker, the local landowner has an extramarital affair with the beautiful show girl, a public hanging, a saloon, a judge... images and archetypes we know from every western with or without John Wayne.

Fascinating the plot then gets because of Dylan's tampering with *time*, much as he does in "Tangled Up In Blue" and "Simple Twist Of Fate": a collage-like series of related impressions, the chronology is interrupted by short atmospheric images and introductions of the main characters.

The Jack of Hearts appears on the scene and turns the head of danseuse Lily, with whom he apparently already shares an amorous past. She is the mistress of the local big shot Big Jim, who is not exactly charmed by Lily's crush. That leads to the climax, which takes place in Lily's dressing room. Big Jim kicks open the door and pulls his revolver, but is stabbed from behind, presumably by his wife Rosemary, whose knees also get weak over the Jack of Hearts. It all comfortably distracts from the work of Jack's gang members, who are prising open the wall of the bank, two doors down. Rosemary is hung the next day, Jack is gone with the booty and the fair Lily is left behind, contemplating.

A cinematic whole, all in all, and indeed two attempts have been made to translate the ballad into a film script. Neither of these scripts has produced a film, unfortunately.

The cinematic and the chosen impressionistic narrative style can certainly be attributed in part to Dylan's recent experiences with Sam Peckinpah, the director of *Pat Garett & Billy The Kid*. That film offers Dylan his first serious acting experience (in the supporting role "Alias") and puts him on the map as a film music composer, when "Knockin 'On Heaven's Door" becomes an acclaimed world hit, but the narrator Dylan has also been paying attention.

Peckinpah is a cyclic narrator; he likes to finish his films at the beginning, and Peckinpah likes to tell choppily, with little time jumps and drawn-out intermezzos - just like Dylan is now shaping his ballad. The story begins and ends in a quiet cabaret, both with the sound of refurbishment work in the background and unfolds with interruptions to introduce the main characters - except for the mysterious Jack of Hearts, who is mentioned in every verse, but about whom we come to know virtually nothing.

Cinematographic qualities also have the words the poet chooses in the descriptive, atmospheric intermezzi. If the camera leaves the action for a moment, having a quick glance at the scene and registering the entry of the judge, it lingers with Rosemary for a while: *Rosemary started drinkin' hard and seein' her reflection in the knife.* Harrowing, foreboding stage direction. It evokes dark premonitions and at the same time the sympathy of the viewer for the cheated Rosemary. Peckinpah could have handled it, such an ominous image, but alas, the director is busy these days, with *Bring Me The Head Of Alfredo Garcia.*

The music colleagues are reluctant to tackle the song. The story comes first, of course, and that slows down the desire to put energy and inspiration in a cover. Although there are dozens of amateur attempts to be found on YouTube, none of them surpasses amateurism.

Among the few professionals there are only two who may reside in Dylan's shadow. Joan Baez first of all, who obviously can claim a kind of property right, or at least a right of use. Her version on the live album *From Every Stage* (1975) has the same big plus as the aforementioned "Diamonds & Rust": beautifully arranged.

The same compliment can be given to Tom Russell, together with Joe Ely and Eliza Gilkyson on the album *Indians Cowboys Horses And Dogs* (2004). Both artists, Baez and Russell, struggle with the length of the song and search for musical solutions to hold attention, to add tension, not to lose momentum. It can often be observed at Dylan covers. A gifted performer like Dylan can repeat the musical accompaniment of any verse from "Tangled Up In Blue" or "Shelter From The Storm" or this *Jack Of Hearts* from beginning to end without any variation; his performance skills do the job. A Tom Russell, for example, is less talented, but has other skills - the ability to dress up the song so well and multicoloured that the music holds the listener (alternating singers, exquisite organ by Joel Guzman).

The artists who fail to do that, who like Dylan do not or hardly vary the musical accompaniment, usually disappoint. Mary Lee's Corvette, the sympathetic Rumpke Mountain Boys... nice, but three minutes is quite enough.

To be fair: even the master himself does not dare to tackle the song live, apart from one unrecorded performance together with Joan Baez, during the Rolling Thunder Revue in 1976. And, of course, that intimate recital from a telephone booth in the Midwest.

8   If You See Her, Say Hello

Bismarck, the capital of North Dakota.

On a freezing January afternoon in 1961, the then sixteen-year-old narrator walks back from school with his best friend and neighbour, Gene. They are overtaken by sirens and flashing lights, heading for Gene's house. Shortly before that Gene's father calmly and determined walked into the local Capitol, the parliament building, shot a popular senator, then walked away quietly, drove home and finally hung himself in the garage. Forty years later, the reason for this horror is still unknown and the narrator goes back in time to resolve that mystery from his youth.

That is the plot of *Sundown, Yellow Moon* (2007), the seventh novel by the American Larry Watson. It is a beautifully chosen title. After a few pages the many fans of Dylan's "If You See Her, Say Hello" get the reference: in the song Dylan sings after these words "I replay the past", just like the narrator intends to do in the novel. It is not a whodunnit, but a why-has-this-happened; just like the narrator in the elegant, gentle song does not question guilt, but is filled with blameless regret. Watson's novels are often visited by Dylan. In this novel at one other occasion, when the narrator remembers that he received a gift from a school friend at the time: *The Freewheelin' Bob Dylan*. In *Laura* (2000) Dylan plays softly on the stereo, in the short story *Redemption* he refers to "The Walls Of Red Wing" and the decors of his works are the late fifties, early sixties in North Dakota, Minnesota and Wisconsin – Dylan country in Dylan time, so to speak.

Dylan will probably appreciate it. In addition, the cinephile Dylan will be pleased that the title of the song even inspires a film. *If You See, Say Hello* is a short, charming actor's movie by Paul Purnell from 2010 for two players, with the title also being the main directional guide. A young woman and a young man are uncomfortably waiting in front of a closed breakfast cafe early in the morning. He wants to talk to her, but does not know how.

And the final scene of episode 5 from the first season is thanks to the song one of the most beautiful scenes from the hit series *Californication*.

Leading actor Hank Moody (David Duchovny) walks on a languid, sunny afternoon with his teenage daughter and dog on the street, by the look of it in Venice, Los Angeles. Daughter experiences her first heartbreak and Moody's first attempt, *La Belle Dame Sans Merci* from Keats, does not bring relief.

> "Is that the best you can do, Dad? How about something from this century?"

That Hank cannot offer, but there is something from the twentieth century. And with the intro of "If You See Her, Say Hello" swelling in the background, he starts to sing, to his daughter's embarrassment. It is a beautiful, moving scene.

The song is one of the triggers to qualify *Blood On The Tracks* as Dylan's "Divorce Album", a genre designation against which Dylan has always resisted. The song does indeed, elegantly and melancholy, say goodbye to a love, but the poet denies the connection with his own marital problems with Sara.

A stroll through his catalog admittedly confirms the counter argument that tender, graceful farewell songs are indeed a constant in Dylan's repertoire. "Girl From The North Country" from 1963, "One Too Many Mornings" and "Mama, You Been On My Mind" in 1964, "Farewell, Angelina" and "Just Like A Woman" in '65 and '66, "I Threw It All Away", "Going, Going, Gone", " Abandoned Love", "We Better Talk This Over", "Most Of The Time"... and that list continues well into the twenty-first century. True, some songs have a bitter or venomous edge. Nevertheless: the theme of *lost love* inspired Dylan to a whole series of melancholy, poignant, poetic lyrics,

It also fits within the long and rich tradition of the *American Songbook*. Dylan listens in these days, as he says, a lot to Joni Mitchell's *Blue*, but undoubtedly Sinatra's *In The Wee Small Hours Of The Morning* (1955) revolves on the turntable, too. "Glad To Be Unhappy", "I Get Along Without You Very Well", the title song, "When Your Lover Has Gone"; all songs in the same mood, songs that Dylan will honour on his "Sinatra albums" in the twenty-first century. "These Foolish Things", "Once Upon A Time", "Somewhere Along The Way", just to name a few - Dylan does have a faible for those gentle songs filled with resigned tristesse.

Within that category "If You Say Her, Say Hello" is an exceptionally successful example. Those songs from the *American Songbook* are beautiful, but lyrically rather one-dimensional, usually. Through a series of similar images or lamentations, one less colourful than the other, the narrator contemplates on a lost love.

The level that the poet Dylan adds to the emotional charge is heartbreaking in all its modesty. Through the absence and the resignation, pain (*it pierced me through the heart*, for example), remorse (*the bitter taste still lingers on*) and self-criticism (*the way I tried to make her stay*) flare up, and thus the poet paints a much richer, multi-faceted, a more moving portrait of the abandoned lover than the overwhelming majority of those farewell songs do.

Mastery is also evident from the harrowing, seemingly inadvertent insertions that manage to express man's loneliness: "She now lives Tangier, *I hear*" and from the sad humility with which he indirectly wraps his hopeless desire for reunification. "Tell her she can look me up, *if she's got the time*", "Don't tell her I still think of her."

The poetic form enforces the strength. "If You Say Her, Say Hello" has no chorus, no refrain, no strict metre - it escapes Dylan's normal conventions for song lyrics and differs from the other songs on the album. It is rather similar to classical poetry, to Great Poets singing a lost love. Petrarch's *Sonnets for Laura*, Goethe's *Marienbader Elegie*, Shakespeare, though less majestic.

The location on the album is also right on target. Of course, a song this strong can stand alone, but here, between the hectic, epic "Lily, Rosemary And The Jack Of Hearts" and the marble, grand masterpiece "Shelter From The Storm", the song gets a calming, intimate added value that makes it all the more piercing.

Dylan has given an unusual amount of love to the final recording. It is one of the five songs he re-records in Minnesota at the end of 1974, during the Christmas holidays. The dazzling, austere version from New York is discarded at the urging of brother David and the song gets dressed up more exuberantly. The lyric changes, stripped of the sharpest edges, make the mild resignation predominant. Musically it now has a beautiful, Mediterranean intro, a slow full-bodied arrangement and a subtle acceleration, making the song seem to work towards a climax. The recording is even edited with a few overdubs, equally unusual with Dylan.

Some mystification in that area does, however, colour the reports about the sessions. Mandolin player Peter Ostroushko would not have been able to play the "butterfly part", the second mandolin part in the high register at the end of song. *Uncut* even reports that "Ostroushko refused to play so high on the neck, because those notes do not come through well." Subsequently Dylan is said to have taken the mandolin, handling it perfectly.

That is a somewhat too dramatic representation of things, but not completely out of order. A first witness, session player Kevin Odegard, is more reliable and reports in his insightful co-production with Andy Gill *A Simple Twist Of Fate. Bob Dylan And The Making Of Blood On The Tracks* (2004) that Ostroushko "for whatever reason" had his doubts about Dylan's wish to also play the same part one octave higher:

> Bob just let it drop, then borrowed the instrument and did it himself. "Nevertheless," Paul Martinson confirms, "Peter's mandolin part is still in there, back in the mix." (The next morning, Ostroushko called his pal Jim Tordoff to tell him all about the "strange dream" he'd had the night before. Tordoff, who had driven Ostroushko from the 400 Bar to the session, cut him off midsentence: "No, Peter, it really happened!")

Incidentally, Peter Ostroushko is a very fine musician, a master on violin, guitar and mandolin on his many solo and duo albums, typically infectious combinations of traditional folk, Eastern European folk music, bluegrass and country.

In later versions Dylan adds yet again sharper, bitter verse fragments. *If she's passin' back this way, most likely I'll be gone / But if I'm not just let her know it's best she stays gone*, for example, and a more sinister variant like *If you make love to her, watch it from the rear / You'll never know when I'll be back, or liable to appear* - biting, vicious lines of verse in which we can hear flashes of the old, mean Dylan from the mid-sixties again.

However, the resigned *Blood On The Tracks* version from Minneapolis remains the standard, also for the many admiring fellow artists who have a go at a cover. Except for the late lamented Jeff Buckley, who sings the New York version on a chilling, lonely, ethereal bootleg recording of a studio session from 1993. *Live At Sin-é* (2003) is really beautiful, too.

Mary Lee's Corvette, obviously, perform the song near-perfectly on the complete cover album *Blood On The Tracks*, 2002, with a surprisingly false slip on *though things get kind of slow*.

The Australian Ross Wilson approaches Dylan's perfection with a driving, crackling version that comes close to the wild mercury sound, thanks to the organ (on an Australian tribute album, *The Woodstock Sessions*, 2000).

One of the most beautiful covers is selected by the master himself, for the film *Masked And Anonymous* (2003) and is the Italian version by the Roman 'Prince of singer-songwriters' Francesco de Gregori, who also receives an honourable mention in the liner notes: "the legend of Italian pop music".

The contribution to the soundtrack is actually rather small. Over the scene in which Jack Fate arrives by bus at his hotel, we hear, roughly glued together, the first forty and the last fifteen seconds. But it encourages Francesco to sing a whole album full of Dylan covers in 2015: *De Gregori Canta Bob Dylan*, with fairly safe, but above all wonderful adaptations.

Translations actually rarely work with Dylan songs, but in Italian everything sounds better, of course. The translation also smoothes the last sharp edges. The pierced heart has been replaced by the sentimental *even though she is no longer here, she is still in my heart* and the bitter taste of the night she left is completely ignored; in that place De Gregori now generously sings that he will not come between her and her new lover.

The Italian turns the yellow moon into an old familiar *"luna blu"*, a blue moon, and presumably for rhyme technical reasons the lady has to move house once again; she no longer lives in Tangier, but further away, in Tunisia. *Se la vedi dille ciao, salutala ovunque sia / E partita tempo fa, e adesso forse e in Tunisia*. Carthago then presumably, where those Romans are not very welcome anymore.

Even the title changes, to *don't tell her it isn't so* - "Non Dirle Che Non È Così". Seems somewhat less catchy than "Se La Vedi, Dille Ciao", but the flair for language of *il principe dei cantautori* is undoubtedly effective.

9   Shelter From The Storm

To today's readers, Charles Dickens (1812-1870) has a sometimes painful preoccupation with physical abnormalities. His novels are teeming with disfigured and flawed people, but at least there is often - but not always - a function. Handicaps with children and the poor elicit a sympathy with the reader (Tiny Tim in *A Christmas Carol* and the faithful, crippled servant Phil Squod in *Bleak House*, for example), with bad guys the body defects serve as external manifestations of inner depravity or as a justified punishment for moral failure.

In *Our Mutual Friend* the parasite Silas Wegg has only one leg, the sycophant Uriah Heep in *David Copperfield* is spastic, the monstrous Quilp (*The Old Curiosity Shop*) is a malicious dwarf with a hump. It is only a small selection; it is a coming and going of canes, crutches, growth disorders, spasms and convulsions at Dickens.

Dickens' letters show that defects and malformations really fascinate him. It looks like he has a tendency to laugh at them - often he mentions a physical defect only to achieve a comical effect. In a letter from 1839 to one W.C. Macready he writes:

> "With the same perverse and unaccountable feeling which causes a heartbroken man at a dear friend's funeral to see something irresistibly comical in a red-nosed or *one-eyed undertaker*, I receive your communication with ghostly facetiousness."

The *one-eyed undertaker* in "Shelter From The Storm" (l. 27) is one of the much-discussed images from one of Dylan's most beautiful songs, but he is never seen as irresistibly comical. Many Dylan fans consider the song a personal favorite and that leads to abundant convictions, unwavering opinions and assertiveness in the Drain of the Western Civilization, in the "discussion groups".

The one-eyed funeral director is a gun and a metaphor for Death. No, a syringe of course, the song is about heroin use. It is "clearly a reference to Bakuu-Met, the one-eyed Persian God of Death". It is the penis and the I-person visits a prostitute. One comic relief still offers, unintentionally, a Flemish analyst:

> "People with one eye haven't got depth-view. They only see two dimensions to exaggerate a little. In everyday -live -outside - intimacy these things/people blow the horn. Undertakers are (in my experience) typically of those one-eyed types."

Jeroen from Antwerp thinks that the word *undertakers* means "entrepreneurs" and thus continues a fine tradition; "We are a nation of undertakers," said a pedantic Dutch prime minister Den Uyl once, in the 1970s, to a group of undoubtedly baffled entrepreneurs from America.

The interpreters with more knowledge of English offer surprisingly often very coherent, but completely divergent interpretations. One sees the song as the monologue of a returning Vietnam veteran or a Holocaust survivor, another as the reflection of a drug addict over his addiction, a third hears the autobiographical wrestling of a husband whose wife eludes him and another recognizes the report of the died soul before the throne of God - and lo and behold, even within the limitation of such a one-dimensional reading, many analysts manage to produce remarkably coherent, line-by-line interpretations.

Agreed, here and there some flexibility is required. God is a woman, in the 1960s being black became a virtue (?) and *not a word was spoken between us* refers to the language barrier between American soldiers and Vietnamese villagers, but apart from a few really desperate jumps, those interpretations are quite fitting. And all of them equally right and wrong, of course. What they have in common is: they trivialise a sparkling poetic highlight by degrading it to *epic*, to a story. In doing so, the exegetes deny the lyrical enchantment of "Shelter From The Storm"; that the song expresses feelings, that the song moves, not because it tells such a catchy or gripping story, but through the beauty of the evoked images of despair, consolation, redemption and hope.

It would also be atypical, in the poet Dylan's oeuvre. He does not do it too often, but if Dylan wants to tell a story, then he is clear about it. He either calls such a narrative song a *ballad* ("The Ballad of Hollis Brown"), or he leaves no misunderstanding about the identity of the main characters ("Hurricane"), or he explicitly mentions the historical event ("Tempest"), or he chooses a cinematic narrative style including direction instructions, dialogues and decor descriptions ("Lily, Rosemary And The Jack Of Hearts").

Characteristic of his lyrical work is the *suggestion* of epic, though. In "Hard Rain" the poet achieves that suggestion by the question-and-answer structure, in "Visions Of Johanna" by opening with a cinematic wide-shot and here in "Shelter From The Storm" by word choice. Subtly inserted signifiers such as "Twas in ...", "up to that point", "suddenly", "now" and "someday" insinuate a linear cause-and-effect story plus summary conclusion, just like the structure of the refrain promises narrative art: *"Come in," she said, "I'll give you shelter from the storm"*. Direct speech, two everyday platitudes (*come in* and *shelter from the storm*), neatly connected by *she said* ... yes, this really does seem to be a patch from some tale.

Incidentally, the textual adjustments and corrections of the poet seem to confirm that he wants to avoid biographical interpretation. In the first versions we hear an extra verse:

> *Now the bonds are broken, but they can be retied*
> *by one more journey to the woods, the holes where spirits hide.*
> *It's a never-ending battle for a peace that's always torn.*
> *"Come in," she said, "I'll give you shelter from the storm."*

"The relation is damaged but can be restored" ... with outpourings like that the writer leaves little room for interpretation, this is getting indiscreet - and that, indiscretion, is precisely what Dylan wants to avoid. It might be true that his marriage with Sara is currently showing surface cracks, but the artist allows reflections only in universal, generally applicable terms. He does not write "confessional songs" and even wants to avoid the suspicion of it - and so he deletes such a verse. The same applies to smaller interventions (changing *she gave me a lethal dose* into *they gave me a lethal dose*, for example).

It does not help, not in the longer term either. To this day, the biographical interpretation, also among professional Dylanologists, is the most popular. And in doing so, son Jakob is always quoted ("I hear my parents talking").

The Vietnam, Holocaust and Second World War interpreters are guided by the first images that the song evokes. They indeed invite to war associations. *Toil and blood* Dylan borrows from Churchill's first speech as prime minister, in The House of Commons on 13 May 1940: *I have nothing to offer but toil, blood and sweat.*

The opening words also have something British; "Twas in another lifetime" reminds of Dickens' opening of *A Tale Of Two Cities* ("It was the best of times, it was the worst of times") and that sublime second line *when blackness was a virtue and the road was full of mud* inevitably summons up war scenes.

In the third line, however, the poet takes a turn to the Bible. Distinctive jargon as "void of form" and "wilderness" comes from Genesis. Again: not to be missed. Already the second line from the Bible is *And the earth was without form, and void* (Gen. 1:2), in the further course of Genesis the term *wilderness* occurs seven times.

Together, it is a chilling portrait of the disheartening emptiness from which the desperate I-person is saved. And that is not all; the song is a necklace with ten sparkling gems - each verse being more beautiful than the next.

The artifice of the first verse, connecting war rhetoric with Biblical idiom, returns a few times, with the same strength. Interpreters of course notice that the first person chronicler identifies himself with Jesus (he wears a crown of thorns, his clothes are gambled away), but again deny the lyrical power of the chosen images: they are metaphors. The protagonist does not say "I am Jesus", but *she took my crown of thorns*, in other words: she eased my pain.

Here and there we see signs that Dylan's associative spirit has led the pen, that he has let the stream of consciousness flow again. *The deputy walks on hard nails* revives "I Walk On Guilded Splinters" from Dr. John, and one of the best known lines, *beauty walks a razor's edge* is a beautiful contamination of Byrons *She walks in beauty* and the expression *walking on a razor's edge*.

Noteworthy is, especially given the classic standing of "Shelter From The Storm", that there still seem to be some errors, both in the official publication of the lyrics (*Lyrics 1961-2012*, for example) and on Dylan's site bobdylan.com. That weird grammatical archaism in *not a word was spoke between us* and the transcription of *futile horn*, in particular. The various studio versions sound more like *feudal horn*, the live version on *Hard Rain* leaves little doubt; Dylan really sings a *d*.

A *feudal horn* does sound a lot tougher, more warlike than a futile horn, of course - although *futile* can also mean 'fruitless, in vain' and then in any case, with respect to content, fits the previous *nothing really matters much*. Remarkable, but not too important. The one-eyed mortician who blows a horn remains an ominous, Hieronymus Bosch-like image either way.

The mythical status of the song does not discourage. Even among the professionals there are dozens of artists having a go at a cover and that is brave. It is a fairly long song, with no variation in the accompaniment (from the beginning to the end the same three chords), so in order to enthral the listener from start to finish, quite a lot of performance skills are required.

Predictably, even the usual suspects fail more often than they succeed. Barb Jungr flees to an unsophisticated jazz arrangement and ditto vocals, Jimmy LaFave does not know how to hold the attention and even Manfred Mann, who often likes to perform the song, is sterile and unimaginative this time.

Much more successful is the version by Rodney Crowell with Emmylou Harris. Sultry, sober and perfectly restrained, but he does cheat a little: Crowell transposes a few couplets to a different key and thus actually adds chords. Forgivable - it is a beautiful rendition, thanks also to Emmylou (on *The Outsider*, 2005).

A division and a lot of speeds lower Steve Adey runs his slow laps. The English minimalist sounds like a copy of John Cale and his dragging covers can turn out to be sleep-inducing, but this hypnotic version of "Shelter From The Storm" works perfectly. On a monotonous sequence of three piano chords, halfway a cello draws long, languid lines and a crisp guitar occasionally sparkles bright accents. Depressing, yes. And very compelling (*All Things Real*, 2006).

The approval of the master himself only Cassandra Wilson receives, even before he has heard her version. In the *Time Magazine* interview with John Farley, September 2001, Dylan sings, unrequited, her qualities:

> "Among the few contemporary acts that excite him is jazz singer Cassandra Wilson. 'She is one of my favorite singers today,' says Dylan. 'I heard her version of Death Letter Blues— gave me the chills. I love everything she does.' He says he would like to see her cover some of his songs."

Cassandra does not give him a chance to change his mind. Immediately on her next album, *Belly Of The Sun* (2002), she performs a chillingly beautiful version of "Shelter From The Storm", full of pent-up suspense, a slightly hoarse, muffled and most of all sensitive, lyrical execution.

Sending enough chills down Dylan's spine to turn him into a Dickens sub-character, undoubtedly.

10   Buckets Of Rain

Leo Kottke is an exceptional world-class guitar player, whose records have led to open mouths and despondency among industrious guitar students since 1969. His singing talents are less skyscraping (in his own words: as "geese farts on a muggy day"), but that is amply compensated by his witty monologues on stage. His chats between the songs sometimes fan out to unfathomable distances and are always very humorous. Kottke has a flawless comical timing, a dry witty presentation and an irresistible, Cleese-like facial expression. At a 2008 concert in Sparks, a suburb of Reno, the master guitarist recounts his meeting with Bob Dylan:

"I met Bob Dylan when he was recording Blood on The Tracks. And I talked to him for about an hour and a half ... but I didn't know it was him. I would have said things ... differently.

There was a book, came out just a couple of years ago, about those sessions. That's how I found out. I got a call from a newspaper in Minneapolis: 'What did you and Bob talk about?' I said: 'Bob who?'

And they told me.

I said: 'I've never met him.'

Well, there were these three witnesses, and these guys were... and I remembered, all of a sudden. This guy, who had walked up, you know, coming up the hall, there were three studios in this building, and he said: 'Well, what do think of this project?' I told him what I thought. And I also raved about everything else, up until then and just about... I was backstage when he played in Denver recently. But I didn't say anything to him."

The book that Kottke is referring to is of course *A Simple Twist Of Fate* by Andy Gill and Kevin Odegaard. That forgotten, long conversation with Kottke is mentioned in passing:

> When Chris and his wife, Vanessa, arrived at the studio, they found Bob in the control room, deep in conversation with celebrated folk guitarist Leo Kottke about a song of Leo's called "So Cold in China," which Bob admired.

The love for that specific Kottke-song Dylan has declared more often. In January 1977, *Melody Maker* publishes a long article about the "Lion Of The Guitar" Leo Kottke, in which Kottke's technician Paul "Shorty" Martinson also speaks. Martinson is also the technician at the Minneapolis re-recordings for *Blood On The Tracks* and tells that he asked Dylan at the time if he had ever heard of Kottke. "Dylan said *yeah* and enthused about a Kottke track, "So Cold In China," on his very first album on the Oblivion label, of which only 1,000 copies were pressed."

The record, Kottke's debut album *12 String Blues* (1969), which was released in an extremely limited edition, has been recorded live in a Minneapolis coffee house, the *Ten O'Clock Scholar*, whereof Dylan will have warm memories. He also played there himself, when he was Robert Zimmerman and that is explicitly mentioned in the liner notes: *Still, as in a now distant past for a younger Robert Zimmerman or John Koerner, the Scholar audience is appreciative and quiet.*

Dylan's enthusiasm for "So Cold In China" probably has more to do with nostalgia or with the creation of the song than with the power of the song itself. It is a beautiful song, no doubt, but it is not so earth-shattering that it would justify Dylan's raving years later. The song has, to him anyway, other charms. Undoubtedly, Dylan read Kottke's own commentary on the song on the cover of that collector's item with interest: "The title and therefore the idea for the song were stolen from someone who sang it in the Ontario Place in Washington, when Mississippi John Hurt was still working there."

It is likely that the encyclopaedicly versed amateur music historian Dylan tells him there in the control room, at that meeting in 1974, from which song Kottke copied the line *So cold in China, the birds do not sing*: from "Long Lonesome Blues", a Blind Lemon Jefferson song from 1926. And that explains Dylan's fascination for a song like "So Cold In China". Lovingly stolen song fragments, patriarchs of the blues like Blind Lemon Jefferson and Mississippi John Hurt, *and,* on top of that, recorded in his own youth club - both the artist and the man Dylan are touched here.

After that witty anecdote, at that concert in 2008, Kottke implores that he has always listened to Dylan *endlessly*, and still does. "Well, now and then", anyway. That confession, and the fact that his heart and the vast majority of his repertoire are rooted in folk music, makes the lack of Dylan covers all the more poignant. One time he takes a shot at one, on "Girl From The North Country", and that interpretation is nice - no more.

However, the real Kottke fireworks could be expected from that one song that is tailor-made for him: the ambivalent, heart-breaking and intimate blues folk "Buckets Of Rain".

It is a beautiful finale to a beautiful record, together with "Desolation Row" and "Sad-Eyed Lady" perhaps the most success-ful swan song in Dylan's discography. After these songs of lost love and despair, the master chooses a melancholic final piece, decorated with confusing, dylanesque contradictions, with naive frankness and inscrutable metaphors. Liner notes writer Pete Hamill partially undervalues the lyrics when he says that it is humorous, "a simple song, not Dante's Inferno", but he does have a point in that the song indeed has the effect of a comic relief, a predominant *but still*-message. The essence of every verse is after all: and yet, in spite of everything, I love you.

In doing so, the poet skims along cutesy teenage poetry. The second verse, for example: a cynical critic will argue that in fact it says no more than *roses are red, violets are blue, but our love will always be true*. And somewhere Dylan also felt a little uneasy. On a bootleg recording of the famous session with Bette Midler (for *Songs For The New Depression*, 1976) apologizes to Midler for the line *I like the way you love me strong and slow* with the words: "I must have written that when I was ten."

It is an unusual and uncommonly harsh comment from the master - and presumably rather prompted by a misplaced outpouring of machismo than by genuine self-criticism. "Buckets Of Rain" brings a balance to *Blood On The Tracks*, gives the nuance precisely by these plain, almost sweet love declarations that so strikingly contrast with the distress. The third verse is the finest example of that disunity; everything about you is beautiful and lovable, and this loss hurts, *everything about you is bringing me misery.*

The poet decorates his outpourings with a melange of idiosyncratic idiom and playful blues quotes. *Meek* Dylan lends from the New Testament, from Jesus' *Sermon on the Mount* ("Blessed are the meek, for they shall inherit the earth", Matthew 5:5). Thus retaining a reference to that sermon. In the beautiful but deleted "Up To Me" the reference is direct ("We heard the Sermon on the Mount and I knew it was too complex"), here Dylan builds a painful antithesis with *meek* on the one hand and *hard like an oak* on the other.

Playful, colourful and impenetrable is the nursery rhyme *Little red wagon / Little red bike*. The little red cart has been rolling through music history for decades. In 1936 Georgia White records "Little Red Wagon", country singer Buddy Jones sings "Red Wagon" in '41, Elvis' great example Arthur Crudup lends the chorus for his own "That's Your Red Wagon" (1945) of which one of Dylan's heroes,

Bob Wills, in 1946 in turn makes the western swing "It's Your Red Wagon". The scholars do not agree on a deeper meaning of that red car. One party suspects a sexual connotation, another explains that the expression means something like *that is your business*. Both interpretations are nonsensical here. Dylan the musician seeks and finds in this verse a nice sounding repetitio, as every verse in this song relies on repetition (*buckets - friends - like - life* and *do*).

For the melody and the rhythm of the lyrics Dylan dives, by and large, a little less deeply into history: the mould for "Buckets Of Rain" has been formed in 1965 and is the popular "Bottle Of Wine" by Tom Paxton, an old comrade from Greenwich Village:

> Bottle of wine, fruit of the vine
> When you gonna let me get sober?
> Let me alone, let me go home
> Let me go back to start over

Paxton is often named in the same breath with Dylan and is just as often recognized as forerunner or even booster of Dylan's career. Not by the least, too. Dave Van Ronk, the "mayor of MacDougal Street", says about him:

> "Dylan is usually cited as the founder of the new song movement, and he certainly became its most visible standard-bearer, but the person who started the whole thing was Tom Paxton ... he tested his songs in the crucible of live performance, he found that his own stuff was getting more attention than when he was singing traditional songs or stuff by other people ... he set himself a training regimen of deliberately writing one song every day. Dylan had not yet showed up when this was happening, and by the time Bobby came on the set, with at most two or three songs he had written, Tom was

already singing at least 50 percent his own material. That said,
it was Bobby's success that really got the ball rolling. Prior to
that, the folk community was very much tied to traditional
songs, so much so that songwriters would sometimes palm
their own stuff off as traditional."

Dylan himself does not deny the influence either. In *Chronicles* he
remembers Tom Paxton as an example of the rare artists who
wrote their own songs, honours one of his most beautiful songs
("The Last Thing On My Mind") and analyses: "Because they used
old melodies for new words, they are well accepted." This trick in
particular inspires the upcoming talent and he will continue to
apply it throughout his career.

Paxton's work also emerges with some regularity. On the *Bootleg
Series 10: Another Self Portrait* we hear that Dylan records Paxtons
"Annie's Going To Sing Her Song" in 1970, in the mysterious poem
An Observation, Revisited from '76 the bard writes under the
pseudonym R. Zimmerman *In my mind I keep hummin' Tom
Paxton's / "Peace Will Come"* and to that song the master also
refers a year later in "Changing Of The Guards" (*Peace will come /
With tranquility and splendor on the wheels of fire*).

And especially in "Buckets Of Rain", for which Paxton's own version
of "Bottle Of Wine" is the model. Not the hit version of that song,
though; the song is known in the driving rock version of The
Fireballs (top 10 hit in 1967), but that one discarded the attractive
guitar plucking which makes Paxton's original and later Dylan's
"Buckets Of Rain" so irresistible.

Countless covers exist of Dylan's gem. YouTube can hardly handle
the stream of enthusiastic living room amateurs. Half of all known
and lesser known singer-songwriters have it on the repertoire and

the number of recordings by experienced artists is endless. In this sea, one thing stands out: a cover of "Buckets Of Rain" is always fun. Apparently, the song has just such a granite, indestructible power as for example "Not Dark Yet" or "Mama You Been On My Mind" - the song is almost impossible to ruin.

Former mentor Dave Van Ronk interprets lovingly and intensely, neighbour Maria Muldaur is sultry, jazzy and slightly vulgar (on her otherwise not very successful Dylan tribute *Heart Of Mine*, 2006) and the *Buckets* of Mary Lee's Corvette unsurpassed venture, the integral version of *Blood On The Tracks*, is one of the many highlights on that album (2002). Grandmaster Jimmy LaFave is by now a *hors concours* (*Road Novel*, 1998, with a beautiful, subdued harmonica part and ditto organ) and that also applies to David Gray, the British prodigy who turns every Dylan cover into an aesthetic masterpiece (*A Thousand Miles Behind*, 2007). Disputed may be the charm of the country twang that Neko Case gives some live versions, but her studio version (on the compilation *Sweetheart: Love Songs*, 2005) is above criticism.

The ladies are doing well either way - in a (questionable) top three, Wendy Bucklew (*After You*, 2002) does belong, too. The male competition up there comes from Iowa: the folk veteran Greg Brown is withered, witty and melancholy - almost at the level of Dylan's original (the same applies to his "Pledging My Time" on *A Nod To Bob Vol. I*, 2001).

But eagerly awaited still is of course Leo Kottke, for that extra dimension: virtuosity.

Headin' for another joint

Record holder is *Another Side Of Bob Dylan*, the album that is recorded in one day, 9 June 1964, in its entirety. But recordings for an album usually don't take much longer anyhow. Dylan is by no means a studio artist, initially hardly values studio production ("It's just a record of songs"), which, moreover, rarely approaches the sound he hears in his head and he proves never-endingly, on stage, that a studio version of a song never is the final version.

He sets aside three afternoons for *John Wesley Harding*, *The Freewheelin'* is done in a few hours, *Planet Waves* is granted six days (and a half). For comparison: Brian Wilson works seventeen sessions on one song, "Good Vibrations", and then has more than seventy hours of music on tape, from which he eventually squeezes a 3:35 minute song. In that same time frame, Dylan records four classic albums, more than sixty songs, and then he still has time left.

The Beatles are for one album, for *Sgt. Peppers Lonely Hearts Club Band*, more than seven hundred hours in the studio - more than Dylan needs for his first twenty (!) studio albums.

Blood On The Tracks is also done quickly and easily. At first, anyway.

In the summer of 1974 Dylan writes fifteen lyrics, half of which will be fully worked out and appear on the album. In the run-up to the recordings, Dylan already seems quite excited about his new songs; in August and early September he plays them to old friends like Mike Bloomfield, David Crosby and Shel Silverstein. And apparently, he is driven by a *back to the roots* sentiment. Dylan contacts the producer of his first albums, his former patron John Hammond. Also, he really wants to record in his old studio, in Studio A of Columbia Records in Midtown Manhattan, on the corner of 52nd Street and 7th Avenue (house number 799), a five-minute walk from Carnegie Hall, where Dylan lives his Renaissance, where he attends Norman Raeben's painting course.

Studio A was sold in 1967 to A&R, to the record company of Jack Arnold and Phil Ramone. But Hammond is a legend, has influence and Phil Ramone is a fan. He already has a click with Dylan - he is behind the decks during the American tour of Dylan with The Band in '74 and is therefore also the recording engineer of the live album *Before The Flood*. One phone call is enough, and the recording starts on Monday 16 September.

In his autobiography *Making Records - The Scenes Behind The Music* (2007), Ramone devotes an entire chapter to *Blood On The Tracks*, although he is not the producer (in fact only the recording engineer; Dylan does not need a "producer" and controls the sound, pace and arrangements of his songs himself).

On Monday morning, a few hours before Dylan arrives, Hammond phones Ramone: could Phil perhaps arrange some musicians? Bob does not want to go back to the roots all the way after all. The original intention, to reduce the songs to vocals, guitar and harmonica, just like on the first albums with John Hammond, has been revised.

Coincidentally, Eric Weissberg is in the studio on Monday morning. Weissberg is a talented guitarist and is currently in the charts with "Dueling Banjos" from the movie *Deliverance*. He is a Dylan fan, delighted with this opportunity and rounds up his music buddies that very same day: Charlie Brown and Barry Kornfeld (guitar and banjo), Richard Crooks (drums), Tony Brown (bass), and Tom McFaul (keys), who then all expectantly report in the studio at the end of the afternoon.

Dylan has arrived earlier and has been tinkering for a while, on his own.

> Now, you've got to understand that Bob Dylan is a bit eccentric: He'll come into the studio and just start playing. And when he does, he concentrates solely on the music. When Bob came in, we got a quick level on him, and he launched into the first of more than a dozen songs.

To some, it probably seemed like Dylan was in his own world.

There was no structure to the session, no feeling that he was being guided or limited by anyone or anything. I didn't yell out, "Ready to roll? This will be Take Two." I'd stopped making those mistakes long before. Attaching numbers to a performance increases the artist's anxiety, however subtly. (...) On these dates, the songs poured out of him as if they were a medley. Bob would start with one song, go into a second song without warning, switch to a third midstream, and then jump back to the first. Bob hardly ever played anything the same way twice, which was disconcerting if you weren't accustomed to it. On the first go-round he'd play an eight-bar phrase; the second time, that phrase would be shortened to six.

In that *stream of consciousness*, as Ramone calls it, Dylan plays "If You See Her, Say Hello", "You're A Big Girl Now" and "Simple Twist Of Fate". His cufflinks are ticking against the guitar body, from time to time the pick scrapes audibly over the microphone, but Dylan does not care and that is something Ramone knows: "I didn't interrupt the performance to correct it." Dylan also plays "Up To Me" and a beautiful "Lily, Rosemary And The Jack Of Hearts".

Until midnight, Dylan and the musicians are working on "Simple Twist Of Fate", "Call Letter Blues" (which changes to "Meet Me In The Morning" at a second take), "Idiot Wind", "You're Gonna Make Me Lonesome When You Go" and "Tangled Up In Blue". It is a dazzling, bizarre experience for Eric Weissberg and his men. While listening back to one take, Dylan is already playing a next song right through it, he gives absolutely no clues, does not even reveal in which key he is playing (and that his guitar is in the particularly unusual open D-tuning) or jumps halfway through the recording to another song.

"Just remember, Eric," Weissberg thinks to himself, "this guy's a genius. Maybe this is the way geniuses operate." Any other session he would have quit already, but luckily Don DeVito is present, the producer who has some experience with Dylan, who has learned from Bob Johnston and who will subsequently take care of Desire, *Hard Rain*, *Street Legal* and *At Budokan*. He has the golden tip: "Watch his feet."

In the end only one recording will survive: "Meet Me In The Morning" - although two days later an overdub is added, the steel guitar by Buddy Cage.

For the last two recordings, Dylan has sent away almost the entire band; he decides to limit himself to acoustic guitars and a bass. It suits. The next day only bass player Tony Brown and organ player Paul Griffin may return.

That next evening, Tuesday, September 17, Dylan starts with "You're A Big Girl Now". The second take, with phenomenal, beautiful, subdued organ playing by Griffin and later added accents by Buddy Cage's steel guitar, is superb and divides the fans to this day: isn't this recording more beautiful, heartbreaking than the one recorded in Minneapolis? Dylan himself is not sure either: for the collection box *Biograph* (1985) he selects this version again.

After a single attempt to record "Tangled Up In Blue", some helpless blues and a "You're Gonna Make Me Lonesome", the three men record two more versions of "Shelter From The Storm", which, despite their undeniable beauty, will be rejected. In 1996 one of these *Shelters* pops up surprisingly: on the soundtrack of the Tom Cruise film *Jerry Maguire*. The fifth verse has different words:

> *Now the bonds are broken, but they can be retied*
> *by one more journey to the woods, the holes where spirits hide.*
> *It's a never-ending battle for a peace that's always torn.*

... words that come across a lot more conciliatory than the revised version from an hour later, selected for *Blood On The Tracks*:

> *Now there's a wall between us, somethin' there's been lost*
> *I took too much for granted, got my signals crossed*
> *Just to think that it all began on a long-forgotten morn*

In between the men struggle with "Buckets Of Rain" and again with "Tangled Up In Blue". It is well past midnight, but the successful *Shelter* has a beneficial effect: the second, faster take on "You're Gonna Make Me Lonesome" is very satisfying - it will eventually be released.

On Wednesday, September 18, Dylan limits himself to four studio hours, during which no definitive recordings will be made, except for the famous overdub of Buddy Cage's steel guitar on "Meet Me In The Morning". The next day, Thursday, September 19, is the last day in Studio A. Only bass player Tony Brown is left and it will be a fruitful day. With Brown, Dylan records the final versions of "Simple Twist Of Fate" and "Buckets Of Rain", the most beautiful version of "Up To Me" and the beautiful "Idiot Wind" which will later surface on *The Bootleg Series 1-3*.

In the following days, the songs are mixed, the song order is determined (the same as on the final album) and the release date is set as December 6. Ramone gives Dylan some acetates, in case he wants to grant family and friends a preview.

Ramone's kind gesture has consequences. Dylan leaves for Minnesota at the beginning of December to spend a few weeks and Christmas with his family. Brother David Zimmerman hears the New York recordings and touches the sore spot: beautiful songs, but they sound quite the same, heard in succession. Dylan, who has been working on the lyrics anyway in the past days, agrees with his brother, calls CBS to postpone the release date and lets his brother arrange studio and musicians for at least a re-recording of "Idiot Wind".

David happens to be the manager of Kevin Odegaard, a commendable singer-songwriter and guitarist who suspects that a performance in 1974 during a wedding of a cousin of the Zimmermans in Lake Minnetonka led to his most famous contribution to pop history:

> Bob had just written and recorded a new song, "Forever Young," that I played. He was sitting about five feet in front of me with his back to me. I gave a very nervous performance, but I think it might have helped lead to an invitation to the *Blood on the Tracks* sessions later that year.

> (interview in *Artful Living,* January 2018)

In 2004 Odegaard, together with the British Dylanologist Andy Gill, writes the rich and insightful book *A Simple Twist Of Fate: Bob Dylan And The Making Of Blood On The Tracks*. The work provides a wonderful insight into Dylan's working method, his eccentric studio behaviour and not leat of all the impact he has on the musicians accompanying him.

In articles and Dylan books, the men from Minnesota are annoyedly often referred to with the somewhat condescending designation *local musicians,* as if Dylan is fiddling around with a few local amateur musicians, up there in Minneapolis. In fact, the men David Zimmerman chooses are experienced to very experienced, professional musicians such as bass player Billy Peterson, drummer Bill Berg, Gregg Inhofer on keys and young talents such as Peter Oustroushko (mandolin, guitar and violin) and Kevin Odegaard. The only amateur who, to his own bewilderment, contributes to the recordings is Chris Weber, the music store owner who lends his precious 1934 0042G Martin guitar, the "Joan Baez model".

When Weber finds out that Odegaard wants to borrow that guitar for Dylan, he seizes the opportunity to see Dylan in real life, and under the guise of "keeping an eye on my expensive guitar", he sneaks himself into the studio.

The ruse succeeds. Once in the studio, Weber gets into conversation with Dylan as he hands him the guitar, both men find a quiet corner and a still charmingly dazed Chris Weber later tells Odegaard, for his book, what happened.

> We chatted for five or ten minutes. He asked me if I played, and whether I wrote anything. I said sure, and he said `Well, play me something you wrote.'

Weber plays an instrumental piece, Dylan is impressed and asks if he also has something with lyrics. The shopkeeper overcomes his captivity and plays a self-written love song, "Come On Home With Me". Dylan is patiently listening the entire song and pays a kind compliment. "That's a nice tune. Linda Ronstadt should do that" (*You can make that happen*, Chris thinks, but he doesn't dare ask).

Then Dylan plays a new song of his own: "Idiot Wind". At that time he apparently already has decided that Weber is skilled enough to act as a sort of intermediary between him and the other musicians - Dylan himself does not want to lose inspiration and drive by first rehearsing a song like "Idiot Wind" with the band. Chris Weber can do that. In the meantime, Dylan and his son Jakob go to see if there is anything good to snatch from the vending machine.

When the band knows the song a little later and technician Paul Martinson has microphones and band ready, Weber can call in Dylan.

> "Dylan walked straight into the vocal booth," says Weber. "There was no guitar set-up in the main room: Everything was baffled off for the bass, drums, and keyboard, and I was a fifth wheel. I hung on to the guitar, figuring maybe I could just sit in the control booth, hang around and listen to the recording session, and he gave me a puzzled look through the glass of the corner booth. I went over and asked if I could stay and listen from the control booth, and he said, *No, man, I need you to play guitar*. I got extremely excited! I'd had no idea that was coming, there was no indication. So I just picked up and played the 1934 0042 on *Idiot Wind*.'

In about five takes it is done and Dylan is very satisfied with the result. So satisfied that he wants to try another song: "You're A Big Girl Now". Bass player Billy Peterson has obligations elsewhere, but the others love to stay. In the same corner Dylan teaches the chord sequence to Weber again; two takes later the song is already done. Dylan himself plays the organ part and flamenco guitar, and that's that.

Back home, Dylan and brother David listen to the recordings a few more times and Dylan gets increasingly enthusiastic. He wants to go again. See if there are any more songs that improve with this approach. David picks up the phone and arranges that they go into the studio again the next Monday, December 30.

It will be a success too. That Monday they first tackle "Tangled Up In Blue", which also undergoes a rigorous transformation lyrically. In his book, Odegaard talks about a musical intervention for which he claims some credit. After he - to his own horror - tells Dylan that the newly recorded version is "passable", an amused and surprised Dylan is curious about Odegaard's ideas to beautify the song.

> "Yeah, it's good," he added quickly, amending his opinion, "but I think it would be better, livelier, if we moved it up to A with capos. It would kick ass up a notch."
> Amazingly, his explanation seemed not only to placate Dylan, but to intrigue him, too. Bob twisted his head, looked around, then down at the floor, musing over the guitarist's suggestion. Finally, he reached a decision, screwing his shoe on the carpet as if extinguishing an invisible cigarette.
> "All right," he said, nodding. "Let's try it."

Dylan must make an effort to reach the higher notes and that, Odegaard says, provides the song the tension, the urgency that (partly) ensures that it has become such an indestructible classic.

There is something to it. Compared to the September recordings from New York, Minneapolis indeed has a pleasantly nervous tension, Dylan's singing is more exciting than in New York and the recording is, indeed, more intense. Or, in the words with which Odegaard sells his suggestion to Dylan: "*It kicks ass up a notch.*"

But there are, obviously, more strong holders to be noted. Foremost Bill Berg's sublime drumming, just as supportive and dynamic as Kenny Buttrey at the time in Nashville on *Blonde On Blonde*, the creative bass playing by Peterson and the *body* the song receives through the twelve-string guitar of the lucky devil Chris Weber.

Dylan too hears the magical power and immediately pushes forward. After "Tangled Up In Blue", the men dedicate themselves to the epic "Lily, Rosemary And The Jack Of Hearts", and the first complete take immediately is solid. Dylan has a harmonica in the wrong key (A instead of D), but the performance is so strong (especially thanks to the Berg / Peterson rhythm section) that a new recording, with the right harmonica that quickly has been fetched from Weber's store, is not needed anymore. Odegaard and Andy Gill argue with rose-tinted hindsight that the wrong key provides a perfect musical counterpoint to the story, but that is quite debatable - that harmonica part is by no means a peak in Dylan's oeuvre.

It is now nine o'clock, so bass player Peterson has to go back to work. After the success of the bassless "You're A Big Girl Now", three days ago, Dylan is curious how "If You See Her, Say Hello" turns out with these men, in this studio, without bass. The delicate, heart-wrenching intro already reveals the answer: the recording from New York is overtaken left and right.

Thus, Minneapolis December 30, 1974 is *Blood On The Tracks'* Royal Warrant holder: three of the ten songs were recorded on that dark Monday in the Sound 80 studio on 2709 East 25th Street, a fifteen minute walk from the Mississippi.

The building currently houses Orfield Laboratories, which converted the studio space into an "anechoic chamber". In 2013 they made the Guinness Book Of World Records - the anechoic room is The Quitest Place On Earth, the place no one can endure for more than half an hour without going out of his mind. With a pain that stops and starts.

11   Call Letter Blues

"But I'm not going to make an album and lean on a marriage relationship. There's no way I would do that, any more than I would write an album about some lawyers' battles that I had. There are certain subjects that don't interest me to exploit. And I wouldn't really exploit a relationship with somebody. (...) So a person in my position says, "Well, I got this available information, this is the way I really feel; I think I'll write it and say how I feel." I don't do that. I don't like feeling those kinds of feelings. I've got to think I can do better than that. It's not going to positively help anybody to hear about my sadness. Just another hard luck story."

(interview with Bill Flanagan, 1985)

To remain discreet is a thing to Dylan, especially in the days when it is rumbling in his marriage, in the days he writes *Blood On The Tracks*. Prior to the above words, he has regretted the indiscrete "Ballad In Plain D" and indirectly admitted that "Idiot Wind" crosses that border, too. But despite his noble intention, the poet Dylan cannot prevent private turbulence, observations, emotions from seeping into his work - he is human, and no man is an island. He is aware of this. In his radio program *Theme Time Radio Hour* (episode 71, Birds) he gives attention, in general, to that mechanism.

A caller from Bloomington, Indiana, has a fundamental question about the song "The Coo Coo Bird" by Clarence Ashley. He wonders what Ashley means by that date, why the singing bird "never hollers coo coo 'til the fourth day of July". What do I know, says the radio host Dylan:

> "If I had to guess, I'd guess it had more do with Clarence Ashley. Perhaps the Fourth of July was important to him for some reason. Maybe it was somebody's birthday, or the day his wife walked out of him. You can never tell why someone's gonna stick something in a song. You just gotta remember that the whole is bigger than the sum of its parts. You can't expect to understand everything in every song."

He may, however, decide not to publish such a trickled in, unwanted indiscretion or to rewrite it. And that seems to have happened with "Call Letter Blues". More radically than ever; Dylan deletes the entire text, writes the words for "Meet Me In The Morning" and sings over the original basic track of "Call Letter Blues". It is a unique manoeuvre in Dylan's output and is probably inspired by his embarrassment about the all too open peep-in, about the verses 2 and 3, which tend to be *exploiting*:

Well, your friends come by for you
I don't know what to say
Well, your friends come by for you
I don't know what to say
I just can't face up to tell 'em
Honey, you just went away

Well, children cry for mother
I tell them, "Mother took a trip"
Well, children cry for mother
I tell them, "Mother took a trip"
Well, I walk on pins and needles
I hope my tongue don't slip

On the other hand: he cannot completely reject the song. Dylan publishes the text in *The Lyrics* (incomplete, oddly enough, only the first four of the seven couplets, just like on the site). And the third, last take of "Call Letter Blues" is selected for the first episode of the acclaimed *Bootleg Series* (1991).

The release of the recording triggers the discussion about the correctness of Dylan's intervention in 1974 and arouses the generally rather senseless exchange of opinions about which song is better. So, in this case: "Meet Me In The Morning" or "Call Letter Blues"?

On *expectingrain.com*, the majority of Dylan fans tend towards *Call Letter* on the relevant discussion forum, while many *Meet Me* voters admit that they prefer "Meet Me In The Morning" for nostalgic reasons; after all, that is the version that they first heard when they were crushed by *Blood On The Tracks*, back in the day.

It is understandable; the magical power of a *56th and Wabasha* alone overshadows the most beautiful couplets of *Call Letter*. But from a distance, without that statistic-polluting nostalgia, the superior class of "Call Letter Blues" is hard to ignore.

The title is already a first great find. Inspired by "Sad Letter Blues" from Tampa Red, presumably, but a *call letter* is the employer letter in which you are offered a job or in which you are invited for a job interview. It is a beautiful, original and twentieth-century metaphor for the supplication of a poor devil who wants to have his wife back home and a beautiful flag on the poetic, refined blues song, which despite its multicoloured nature is more coherent than "Meet Me In The Morning".

In terms of content, it is a variant on the song from which it also borrowed the structure, on "32-20 Blues" by Big Maceo from 1945 (with Tampa Red on guitar) and on the motif of the murderous cuckold at any rate. The poet Dylan, however, incorporates that motif infinitely more elegantly than the many straightforward classics from the decades before. There, it usually is presented with the subtlety of the sledgehammer:

> *I walked all night long with my 32-20 in my hand*
> *I walked all night long with my 32-20 in my hand*
> *Lookin' for my woman, while I found her with another man*

... as Big Maceo sings in that "32-20 Blues". Robert Johnson does not like mistiness either, in the eponymous, much-covered classic, which is also on Dylan's repertoire:

> *And if she gets unruly, thinks she don't wan' do*
> *If she gets unruly and thinks she don't wan' do*
> *Take my 32-20, now, and cut her half in two*

Still, neither of these men, Big Maceo nor Robert Johnson, and indirectly Dylan, did invent it. Back in 1929, Robert Sykes recorded the bloodthirsty "44 Blues", with the opening lines that will end up in "Call Letter Blues" via Big Maceo:

> *Lord, I walked all night long with my forty-four in my hand*
> *Lord, I walked all night long, my forty-four in my hand*
> *I was lookin' for my woman, found her with another man*

A year later Sykes also writes a "32-20 Blues" (same title, but another song than Maceo's and Johnson's) and is also pretty clear:

> *Lord, I carry my 32-20 in my right hand*
> *Lord, I carry my 32-20 in my right hand*
> *Lord, I'll shoot my woman 'bout wastin' time with a monkey man*

It always has been and continues to be a popular motif throughout the ages, the bloody revenge of the deceived lover. It appeals to a millennia-old moral sense and is legitimized early in the Old Testament, in Leviticus 20: *And the man that committeth adultery with another man's wife, even he that committeth adultery with his neighbour's wife, the adulterer and the adulteress shall surely be put to death.*

Half of the opera repertoire relies on the *crime passionnel*, in the judiciary it is a mitigating circumstance, it is an evergreen in Hollywood and in the pop music from The Beatles ("Run For Your Life", 1965) to Rihanna ("Man Down", 2011). But never as fragile, as suggestive as in "Call Letter Blues".

The prelude is pastoral. A lonely soul walks the streets at night and seeks solace in the distant sounds of church bells. Intriguing is the cliff hanger: he wonders whether those bells are ringing for him, for something he would have done wrong.

The solitude, we understand in the second verse, is involuntary. His wife has left him. Not only him, tells verse three, the children miss their mother too and he does not know what to say, he is lying about a holiday trip, he bites his tongue: *I walk on pins and needles and I hope my tongue don't slip*. It occupies him in a sheer neurotical way. Every time someone walks past their house, he jumps up. Is it she? Is she back? Only then, in the fifth verse, we learn that there is another man in play. But this wretch is the meek opposite of all those gun-wielding, violent blues heroes. I know you're with another man, but that's alright. You know I always understand. A comforting escape to carnal, physical love is within reach, he walks along the harlots, they are all free ... but the grief is too overwhelming, his head is not there.

So far it already is an original, layered variation on all that murderous *My Baby Left Me* whining from the blues canon. This narrator is not aggressive, aggrieved, unreasonable. He does not want revenge, he is gentle and forgiving, and wants to save his children grief.

But then the last verse.

> *My ears are ringin'*
> *Ringin' like empty shells*
> *My ears are ringin'*
> *Ringin' like empty shells*
> *Well, it can't be no guitar player*
> *It must be convent bells*

Ringing ears, "like empty [bullet] shells", and that is due to the death bells of the monastery; we now get the answer to that riddle in the first verse, where the church bells are ringing, "maybe because I've done something wrong".

The mild, lenient narrator is either a confused, or an intelligent psychopath, at least a man who knows how to conceal, fully credible, that he has just shot down his adulterous wife - perhaps because he does not even remember it.

It is a pioneering, literary version of all those revenge songs that "Call Letter Blues" elaborates on. In those songs the firearm violence is usually announced in the first or second verse. The narrator swings his 32-20 (the .32-20 refers to the 32 caliber Winchester bullet with a load of 20 grains, about one and a half grams, gunpowder), his German Luger ("Down In Spirit Blues", Tampa Red), his razor, rifle and Gatling machine gun ("Georgia Hound Blues", also from Tampa Red) or his .44 (Roosevelt Sykes means his .44 Winchester, "the gun that won the West").

Similarly, Dylan's forerunners are painfully clear about what they are planning to achieve with those tools ("shoot my lady", "kill my baby", "she's dead and gone"), but this protagonist surprises us with his murderous mood, and then still only indirectly; through that unusual, lugubrious empty bullet shell metaphor and that reference to the church bells, he only hints, in the very last verse only, that there is blood on his tracks.

The church bells metaphor is just as classic, and in this song just as suggestive and indirect as the firearm violence. On his debut album Dylan covers already the evergreen "See That My Grave Is Kept Clean":

> *Did you ever hear them church bells tone*
> *Means another poor boy is dead and gone*

... like death bells sound in dozens of blues songs, and they always mean that these bells are ringing because my baby is dead. The Mississippi Sheiks in "Stop And Listen Blues" (1929), Muddy Waters in his "Buryin' Ground Blues" (1947), "Sad And Lonely Day" by Roosevelt Sykes (1933) and also Dylan himself sometimes chooses the explanatory addition. In "Standing On The Doorway" for example, and in "Can't Escape From You":

> *The dead bells are ringing*
> *My train is overdue*
> *To your memory I'm clinging*
> *I can't escape from you*

But in "Call Letter Blues" words like *dead*, or *gone*, or *no more* do not occur; just like the empty bullet shells, these clocks only insinuate a macabre background.

The poet Dylan produces here, in short, a veiled literary thriller superior to "Romance In Durango" (*Desire*, 1976) to "Señor" (*Street Legal*, 1978), to "Man In The Long Black Coat" (*Oh Mercy*, 1989), reaching a level he will not achieve again until "Soon After Midnight" (*Tempest*, 2012): so very, very much more than *just another hard luck story.*

12   Up To Me

It is a beautiful melancholic title, the title of Richard Fariña's only novel: *Been Down So Long It Looks Like Up To Me* (1966). He did not make it up himself, but borrowed it from a song by the early blues giant Furry Lewis, from "I Will Turn Your Money Green".

With Fariña's traveling companion Dylan, the song also echoes through, albeit some decades later. The second verse of "Tryin' To Get To Heaven" (*Time Out Of Mind*, 1997) opens with *When I was in Missouri / They would not let me be* - the opening lines of the same "I Will Turn Your Money Green".

Richard Fariña is a short, well-nigh cinematic and almost mythical intermezzo in Dylan's life. The dropout student English is already around in Dylan's circles in the early 1960s. The men meet when Richard is still married to the popular folk singer Carolyn Hester (Dylan plays harmonica on her third album, in 1961). They become friends and the friendship gets an extra layer when Fariña remarries in '63 with Joan Baez's beautiful sister, the then seventeen-year-old, enchanting Mimi. That happiness does not last long; April 30, 1966, two days after the publication of his only novel, Richard is killed in a motorcycle accident in Carmel Valley, California, on a borrowed bike.

The book by David Hajdu, *Positively 4th Street: The Lives and Times of Joan Baez, Bob Dylan, Mimi Baez Fariña, and Richard Fariña* (2001) is a comprehensive and occasionally somewhat maudlin historiography about the lives of the foursome, especially about those years in which that special carom of creative talent around the sisters Baez takes place. Hajdu is rather stuck in the debatable conviction that Fariña was the real creative genius and Great Guide, but nevertheless the work offers a rich look at Dylan's years with Baez, documented, among other things, with revealing and candid letters from Baez's private correspondence.

That song by Furry Lewis is not the only line that can be drawn between "Up To Me" and Fariña. The title similarity between Dylan's song and Fariña's novel is evident, and besides that the lyrics also offer small references. *Thunderbird* is also the name of the bookstore where Fariña has a signing session a few hours before his death, the second line, *Death kept followin', trackin' us down*, recalls the two motorcycle accidents where one (Fariña) finds death and the other, Dylan, escapes. And with some lenient interpretation, there are some lines of verse which can be read as a reply to Fariña's farewell salute to Bob Dylan, the bittersweet song "Morgan The Pirate".

That song is released posthumously, on the album *Memories* (1968). The liner notes on that album are usually mistakenly attributed to Mimi, but they are written by Maynard Solomon, producer and founder of Baez's record company Vanguard. The notes claim that this song is Fariña's last song and "waves farewell to Bob Dylan".

In the lyrics, sung by Mimi over an up-tempo folk-rock song propelled by electric guitars, the melancholy seems to dominate, but through the melancholy Richard administers some quite nasty blows:

> *It's bye bye buddy have to say it once again*
> *I appreciate your velvet helping hand*
> *Even though you never gave it I am sure you had to save it*
> *For the gestures of the friends you understand*
> *Now you've gotten even higher*
> *And become your own supplier*
> *And the number one denier of the one or two hard feelings*
>
> *One or two hard feelings left behind*

In this last verse the poet suggests that he loses Dylan to the drugs, in the verses before he accuses him of opportunism, disloyalty and deceiving the public.

Sir Henry Morgan, Morgan the Pirate (1635-1688), was one of the most successful pirates in the service of the English Navy and the terror of the Spanish Empire in the Caribbean. A link with the lyrics is hard to find and why Fariña names a song about Dylan after the legendary buccaneer, is puzzling too. Because he considers Dylan a marauder, song stealer, thief of thoughts? Maybe they went to the movie (1960) together.

If the song has made some impression on Dylan, then not so much that he has written a clear reply to it. But, as with any artist, reflections and resonances from the man's life creep into his work. At any rate, the protagonist in "Up To Me" defends himself against the kind of accusations as expressed in "Morgan The Pirate"; *if I'd lived my life by what others were thinkin', the heart inside me would've died* and the following *I was just too stubborn to ever be governed by enforced insanity.*

Too thin, all in all, to classify "Up To Me" as an answer song, but that the song expresses a confetti rain of private concerns from a reflective narrator, that much is obvious.

Those reflections also invite to look for lines to Dylan's biography and can be found indeed. Especially that last verse, of course:

> *And if we never meet again, baby, remember me*
> *How my lone guitar played sweet for you that old-time melody*
> *And the harmonica around my neck, I blew it for you, free*
> *No one else could play that tune, you know it was up to me*

... which is at least a retrospective on a past love relationship and is thankfully abused by most of the exegetes as a further 'proof' that *Blood On The Tracks* thematises Dylan's marital problems and upcoming divorce.

Here too, however, love affairs in the life of the private person Dylan undoubtedly belong to the many impressions that one way or the other trickle down into his artistic output. But Dylan does not write songs à clef or confessional poetry. Masterpieces like "Tangled Up In Blue", "Simple Twist Of Fate" or this "Up To Me" are much more facetted than that.

Narrative "Up To Me" also *appears*, but unlike those seemingly epical songs on *Blood On The Tracks*, this song starts *in medias res*, in the middle of an action. Not "early one morning, the sun was shinin'" nor "they sat together in the park as the evening sky grew dark", but wham-bam: *everything went from bad to worse, money never changed a thing.*

The style figure contributes to the cinematic character of the song. In the literature, such an opening without an introductory exhibition can be found often enough (*Paradise Lost* by John Milton, Shakespeare's *Hamlet*, Edgar Allen Poe in *The Tell-Tale Heart* and equally in the epic poetry of classics such as Homer and Virgil), but it is much more common in the film noirs and thrillers. *The Usual Suspects* (1995), *Kill Bill* (2003), and especially in the crime films from the 40s and 50s. As in almost every film Dylan mentions in his autobiography *Chronicles*.

"Joe, you're under arrest" is the opening of *Rio Bravo* (1959). *The Defiant Ones* (1958) opens with the singing of someone in the back seat, out of view, and in the front the driver says to the co-driver: "Will you listen to him? We oughta make him ride up front. See how much singin' he'll do then."

The stranger, the protagonist Sidney Poitier, sings W.C. Handy's "Long Gone" from 1920, a song that he will sing a few more times. The film seems to be summed up in the first verse of "Up To Me" and the song "Long Gone" gets a name-check (*I know you're long gone, I guess it must be up to me*).

And in the middle of the story starts *La Strada* (1954), so admired by Dylan:

> *Gelsomina! Mother says to come home right away. There's a man here. He came on a big motorcycle. He says Rosa is dead.*

The second big difference with the epic songs on *Blood On The Tracks* is the lack of a continuous storyline; not only the song itself, all twelve verses of "Up To Me" are equally abrupt ouvertures of film scripts, of film noirs, romantic dramas and psychological thrillers. The suggestion of a continuous storyline is there, sure. The protagonist is a retrospective I-figure in all twelve stanzas, the poet sprinkles reference words and indicative pronouns that seem to refer back to something that was told in a previous verse, conjunctions at the beginning of the verse insinuate that a thought from a previous verse is continued (*"And"*, *"So"*).

However, it is only the *suggestion* of a plot. Unlike in the twin sister of "Up To Me", in "Shelter From The Storm", no comprehensive, coherent picture looms up; "Up To Me" appears to consist of puzzle pieces of twelve different puzzles, where at most - with some difficulty - one can distinguish "farewell" or "love break" as the overarching theme in ten of the twelve verses. The evoked images push the associations like a flaring pigeon swarm in all directions, and the images do not group themselves. Perhaps this song is the song that Dylan thinks about when he makes a mystifying point in *Chronicles*:

> "Eventually I would even record an entire album based on Chekhov short stories – critics thought it was autobiographical – that was fine"

Probably a red herring, but true: blooming orchids, departing trains, a stale perfume smell, an officer's club and an unhappy lover waiting outside all night ... many images from "Up To Me" could just be borrowed from Chekhov's stories. Though still slightly off: stale or attenuated smells are recurring at Chekhov, but it is always the stale smell of tobacco or cigars. Perfume is always "enchanting", "intoxicating" or "penetrant". Orchids are not mentioned in any work, nor an officer's club, no bluebirds or post office workers, only nightly languorous, unfortunate lovers sometimes do come along - but then again, that would apply to half of the world literature.

No, this is not a "song like a painting", a song whose parts tell a different story than the whole. Only the music itself and the protagonist hold it together, but establishing a larger whole remains guesswork.

It does not detract from the beauty. The twelve miniatures contain beautiful one-liners (*when you bite off more than you can chew you pay the penalty*), enigmatic sub-characters (*the old Rounder in the iron mask slipped me the master key*), the softest put-down in Dylan's catalogue (*she's everything I need and love but I can't be swayed by that*) and intriguing musings with beautiful metaphors.

"We heard the Sermon on the Mount and I knew it was too complex / It didn't amount to anything more than what the broken glass reflects." The Sermon on the Mount complex? He can hardly mean Jesus' Sermon on the Mount – that one excels in plain language and clear messages. The opposite of Dylan's "Up To Me", actually.

The verses are larded with half-known, sometimes archaic expressions that the poet picks from ancient songs, forgotten films and classical poetry. A *rounder* is an extinct expression for a vagabond, a designation we only know from old songs ("Cocaine Blues", "Delia", "Lady And The Tramp", from songs by Dylan's old heroes like Dock Boggs and Blind Willie McTell).

The verse with "Dupree" and "Crystal" in the "Thunderbird Café" sounds like the plot of a Tennessee Williams movie adaptation and the "bluebird" is sung in hundreds of songs, but the concept of the blue bird of happiness who is singing in this song , comes from the play *L'Oiseau blue* (1908, adapted for film seven times, so far) by that other Nobel Prize winner, by Maurice Maeterlinck.

In short: "Up To Me" is one more of those sparkling, chameleonic Dylan songs from the hors category in which we also classify songs like "Desolation Row", "Things Have Changed" or "Not Dark Yet". *And* one of those songs in which we recognize the artistic kinship with fellow Nobel laureate T.S Eliot, with the cut and paste in a masterpiece like *The Waste Lands*. "A heap of broken images", as T.S. puts it in line 22 of that work.

The overall consensus on why Dylan passes this masterpiece for *Blood On The Tracks* is: it is too similar to "Shelter From The Storm".

The first official release of Dylan's recording is in 1985 for the *Biograph* collection box. In the accompanying booklet, Cameron Crowe writes: "A companion piece to *Shelter From The Storm*, performed in the same spare style." And Crowe also sees the final verse as "proof" that Dylan is autobiographical here, but Dylan himself closes that comment off, with the rebuttal we often hear: "I don't think of myself as Bob Dylan. It's like Rimbaud said: *I is another*."

Much earlier we have already been able to get acquainted with the song in the version of Roger McGuinn. Dylan gives his old friend the song for his most beautiful solo album, *Cardiff Rose* (1976), on which it is also, despite all the beauty surrounding it, the highlight. The ex-Byrd opts for an electric, very lively, almost enthusiastic country-rock approach and proves once again that he has the rather rare skill to raise a Dylan song. Or maybe even more so: producer Mick Ronson does. Both men have just toured with Dylan, with the *Rolling Thunder Revue*, and from there they also take back to the studio star musicians Rob Stoner, Howie Wyeth and David Mansfield, to record *Cardiff Rose* in Los Angeles.

During that tour, the remarkable talent Ronson has already shown that he can give especially successful, enriching twists to Dylan songs (to "Going, Going, Gone", for example). Here, with the enormous influence that he has as a producer and multi-instrumentalist (Ronson plays guitar, zither, flute, piano, organ, percussion and accordion), he can perfectly decorate such a Dylan

BLOOD ON THE TRACKS

song to his taste. Successful, undeniably; even unyielding Nobody-Sings-Dylan-Like-Dylan zealots nod thriftily, but approvingly to this cover.

The only other cover that comes close to this one is from Roger McGuinn again. In the twenty-first century he records a folky, hypnotic version of "Up To Me" for a tribute album (*Dylan Covered*, Mojo Magazine September 2005). More monotonous and acoustical then his pièce de résistance from thirty years earlier and again close to the beauty of Dylan's original - even without Ronson McGuinn can deliver a masterpiece.

The first crow of the rooster

In 1979, the Guinness Book Of World Records officially recognized the Shortest Interview in the World, an interview conducted during a Dylan concert by *Creem* journalist Jeffrey Morgan, who is in the front row at the time of the "interview".

> Dylan: This next number is a song I once did with the Band. You remember the Band, don't you? It was on an album called Planet Waves. It sold twelve copies.
> Morgan: WHY?
> Dylan: Get this guy outta here.

It's October 1978, and Dylan makes that sour joke almost every night. With increasing sales figures, by the way; the first time there are only four sold (October 5, in Maryland), two days later already six, October 9 reports Dylan: "About ten of them have been sold. Ha, it sells better every day," and the sales record is then set in Toronto on October 12, when there are no fewer than twelve copies sold.

He always says it halfway through the evening, with the announcement of "Going, Going, Gone", one of the two songs from *Planet Waves* he performs that evening (the other is "Forever

Young"). The acidity is not entirely justified, but it is understandable. In the presale the album broke Dylan's record; more than half a million orders, enough for gold and the first place on the Billboard 200. After the release, however, sales stagnate, despite the - generally - positive reviews and the sold-out tour with The Band. A year later, on top of that half a million, "only" a hundred thousand extras were sold. That initial success is mainly due to the excitement that the first real Dylan album in four years has been generating, not so much to the earth-shaking quality of the album - there won't be too many fans among whom *Planet Waves* is in the Top 10 of best Dylan albums.

Even super fan Patti Smith withdraws. She will never belittle anything from her hero, but in her review (*Creem*, April '74) she does take some sort of distance. "I've been following him like a good dog for too long now," Smith writes, judging that the album is unbalanced, that The Band makes her nervous and that she is not very touched by the album, except for two songs: "I don't care for the rest of the album."

The two songs that fully justify the purchase of *Planet Waves* are the opposite of each other, Smith argues poetically. "Dirge" and "Wedding Song".

> "One black one white. One that swan dives and one that transcends. The death of friendship the birth of love. It's a thin line between love and hate."

The black one, Smith explains just to be sure, is "Dirge." And she loves the musical accompaniment, the lyrics and especially the contrast with the white one, with "Wedding Song". But "Dirge" she plays over and over. And well alright, "Going, Going, Gone" has beautiful lyrics and should be covered by Mick Jagger or Chuck Jackson.

The discomfort of Smith and many other reviewers mainly concerns the homeliness, the valentines and roses, the cosiness of most lyrics. The fans and the reviewers, in varying degrees of aversion, have been bothered by that since the final two songs on *John Wesley Harding* from 1967 ("Down Along The Cove" and "I'll Be Your Baby Tonight"), it gets worse by the hundred percent score of unpretentious songs on successor *Nashville Skyline* ('69), with a *crooning* Dylan, to add insult to the injury, sung without any overtones of sarcasm or cynicism, and the embarrassment reaches the top of the end on *New Morning* (1970), with sweets like "If Not For You ", skyrocketing confessions such as *this dude thinks you're grand* (from "Winterlude") and rural warblings as in "Sign On The Window" (*Marry me a wife, catch a rainbow trout / Have a bunch of kids who call me "Pa" / That must be what it's all about*).

Now, completely evaporated it has not. The fans and critics still miss Dylan's razor sharpness, his venom and his uppercuts, in "On A Night Like This", "Hazel", "Something There Is About You" and "You Angel You". But some light on the horizon bring the instant classic "Forever Young", the intense "Never Say Goodbye" and the irresistible "Tough Mama". But most plus points are given to the two songs that are the harbinger of *Blood On The Tracks*, the songs demonstrating the deep truth of Dylan's own adage from "She's Your Lover Now" (1965): *pain sure brings out the best in people*.

Those two songs are the same songs Patti Smith picks out: "Going, Going, Gone" and "Dirge".

13   Going, Going, Gone

It is still standing there, the auction block on which the slaves had to stand to be sold by auction, on the corner of Charles and William Street in Fredericksburg, Virginia. Controversial enough, to many Fredericksburgers, but on September 26, 2017 the city council, after heated discussions, decides that the historical interest outweighs the weight of the shame. The block and memorial plate remain in place, the *Olde Town Butcher* has to swallow that bitter symbol of inhumanity right in front of his shop door.

The practice of slave auctions has been immortalized in the song "No More Auction Block", a song that surfaced somewhere in the middle of the nineteenth century. Origin is unknown, but we know that it was sung as a march song by the so-called *Black Regiments* during the American Civil War (1861-65). A decade later the legendary Fisk Jubilee Singers travel around with that song on the repertoire and a century later it is still on the setlist of black artists - Odetta, in particular, keeps it alive. Dylan sings it one time, in 1962, and then knocks up the melody for "Blowin 'In The Wind", which he will perform a bit more often.

Dylan will never again sing about slave auctions, but a derivative inspires one more time: *going, going, gone* is the formula with which the auctioneer closes the deal. It is a gripping, charged and rhythmically strong catchphrase. Dylan also has found a beautiful melody, but lyrically it does not really work. His approach becomes clearer only later, after the many text revisions: it is meant as a resigned lament of a faded love, of a lover who recognizes that he has to put an end to it.

But then, we are in those dry and barren years 1969-73, the years in which the poet Dylan is watching the river flow, waiting for the inspiration for a masterpiece to bubble up again. After that successful find for the chorus, it will stagnate again; *text* rhymes with *next*, *edge* with *ledge*, a couplet is helplessly closed with an empty line like *it's the top of the end*... no, this is not the poet of majestic masterpieces like "Visions Of Johanna" and we are still waiting for the genius of "Up To Me" and "Tangled Up In Blue". And ambiguity usually does not concern Dylan, but this time he is apparently annoyed by the consensus among reviewers and fans that this song is so poignant, so bleak, the conviction that the narrator is going to end his life here.

This view is indeed obvious. The images from all four couplets one associates with an end of life rather than with a love ending: "the willow does not bend", "the book is closed", "I hang on a thread" and "I am standing on a ledge" ... and then there is the chorus with that ambiguous *gone*, which of course can also mean "passed away, deceased".

That is not the idea. At the first live performances (Rolling Thunder Revue II, from April 18, 1976), Dylan has already done a lot of reworking. A *you* is introduced, that scary ledge has been deleted and the whole rewritten last verse makes the whole song leaning much more on *heartbreak*:

> *I'm in love with you baby*
> *but you got to understand*
> *that you got to be free*
> *so let go of my hand*

In the ten 1976 performances Dylan will stick to this variant. With small deviations, though; Joan Baez comes along on this tour and sings four times her beautiful, melancholy ode about her past relationship with Dylan, "Diamonds And Rust". It entices the sung person to a teasing wink back. At the end of May, in Texas, Dylan shuffles words, phrases and couplets in "Going, Going, Gone" and adds:

> *I've been sleeping on the road*
> *with my head in the dust*
> *Now I just got to go*
> *before it's all diamonds and rust*

These lyrical adaptations, and the fact that Dylan usually presents flaming, aggressive performances of the bitter "Idiot Wind" after the song, feed the thought that the man Bob Dylan vents personal concerns, that the lyrics are an autobiographical expression of love or marital problems. This conviction gets an extra boost after the next text revision, the one for the performances during the Far East Tour, February and March 1978. Now there is no doubt whatsoever about the source of man's misery – love issues, not life issues. The opening verse immediately puts things in order:

Well, I've just reached a place
where I can't stay awake
I got to leave you baby
before my heart will break
I'm going, I'm going, I'm gone

And the following verses stress the message, with the poet harking back to the country idiom of "Tonight I'll Be Staying Here With You" and "I'll Be Your Baby Tonight", but now with an opposite content:

Fix me one more drink baby
and hold me one more time
But don't get too close
To make me change my mind

Finally, Dylan underlines that he does not use *going going gone* in a metaphorical, morbid sense, but literally: this man takes up his suitcase and leaves. We now even know where:

Now from Boston to Birmingham
is a two day ride
But I got to be going now
'cause I'm so dissatisfied

Some twelve hundred miles, a two day ride, indeed. Why the poet chooses these two cities is probably not very relevant. Boston stands for Northern, intellectual, worldly, cultural and Birmingham, Alabama is associated with the South, and then with the negative cliché images of it; rednecks, provincial narrow-mindedness, racism and backwardness. She lives in Boston and he is from Birmingham - it illustrates incompatibility, an impossible relationship, something like that.

But maybe the poet only looked at his tour schedule. At the end of September '78 Dylan plays in Boston, *a two months ride* later, early December in Birmingham.

In the last version, from the Europe summer tour '78, Boston and Birmingham have already been eliminated and old fashioned blues idiom finds its way in:

> *I've   been   hanging   round   your   house   so   long*
> *You   been   treating   me   like   a   clown*
> *You   haven't   done   nothing   but*
> *tear a good man's reputation down*

Pretty literal from Robert Johnson's "From Four Until Late" (*From four 'till late, she get with a no-good bunch and clown / Now, she won't do nothin', but tear a good man's reputation down*).

Improvements, all of them, but they do not last. After 1978, Dylan never plays the song again, covers always follow the original lyrics on *Planet Waves* and in the liner notes of *Trouble No More* (2017) the celebrated music journalist Amanda Petrusisch is unaffected, insisting persistently   that Dylan likes to write about death, sometimes "in obvious ways, in songs like *Going, Going, Gone* and *Knockin' On Heaven's Door*". Back to square one.

The real strongholder of the song, the music, grows along with the lyrical improvements. It's already one of the highlights on *Planet Waves*. An intro is never better than here and Robbie Robertson's guitar with those pinched notes generates goose bumps, but the *Rolling Thunder* version still exceeds that. The influence of the brilliant music producer and rock guitarist Mick Ronson is audible.

He is the man whose arrangements elevate Bowie's songs on *Hunky Dory* and *Ziggy Stardust* and Lou Reed's songs on *Transformer* to timeless classics. The magistral strings arrangement of "Life On Mars?" is his, for example, "Satellite Of Love" and "Perfect Day" are beautiful songs but become pop monuments only when Ronson shapes them.

Apparently, he has shed his light on "Going, Going, Gone" and turns it into an incredibly exciting, dramatic rocker. The "You Really Got Me"-like hook behind the lines is a brilliant addition and contrasts beautifully with the whirling, lyrical accompaniment under the verse lines before and after, repeating the bridge, before the last verse, indeed gives the song extra body and the alternation of the slightly chaotic instrumental intermezzos with the tighter, barren arrangement between the sung parts provides an irresistible added depth.

Self-interest, presumably. From Mick Ronson is also the illustrious quote "Actually, I never liked Dylan's kind of music before; I always thought he sounded just like Yogi Bear" - so he turns the songs a bit more into his own taste.

More colleagues follow that example. Veteran Bettye LaVette is seventy-two years old when she surprises with the very successful tribute album *Things Have Changed* (2018). Her twelve interpretations of Dylan songs, and especially of neglected songs like "Seeing The Real You At Last" and "Political World", lead to praising and jubilant reviews worldwide. The album closes, after a steamy, driving "Do Right To Me Baby", with a dreamy, intimate "Going, Going, Gone".

Flashing, but not as overwhelming as the most beautiful cover of the song. Gregg Allman records a full album shortly before his death (May 2017), *Southern Cross*, for which he once again did everything with producer Don Was. Initially, Allman wants to say goodbye with an album filled with original, own songs. The preliminary title even was *All Compositions By Gregg Allman*. This does not work out, mainly because of his health problems (liver cancer) and he then decides to cover songs that mean a lot to him. Obviously, Gregg sees "Going, Going, Gone" also as a gripping farewell to life, too.

Never mind. Allman's version is heart-breaking, swampy and soulful - the South of the slave trade and the auction blocks emerges again.

14   Dirge

In March 2015, Dylan's publisher Simon & Schuster publishes Shane Dawson's *I Hate Myselfie*, a memoir in which the popular YouTube vlogger dwells on eighteen of his most embarrassing events. It is a bit of a juvenile, sophomoric work, but still (or: therefore) a success, a New York Times bestseller and the umpteenth example in a long, long line of authors who exploit self-loathing literarily.

That Italian poet from the fourteenth century, Petrarca, composes in *Canzoniere 134* "*ho in odio me stesso, e amo altrui*, I hate myself and love another," Kafka's oeuvre is one long exercise in self-hatred, with *Brief an den Vater* ("Letter To His Father") as a climax (or low point, depending how you look at it), the posthumously published *Journals* by Kurt Cobain can only be read as a run-up to his suicide and even Erasmus thinks that self-love is a moral sin; the true Christian is characterized by self-hatred (*Handbook of a Christian Knight*, 1503).

And a prominent place in Dylan's record collection is occupied by
Tampa Red, the blues wizard who records "I Hate Myself" in 1936,
with the opening lines that inspire:

> I hate myself for falling in love with you
> 'Cause you wrecked my life
> And you broke my heart in two

From this perspective, Dylan joins a long tradition when he opens
"Dirge" with *I hate myself for loving you*. But there is a big
difference: with Petrarca, Kafka and Cobain, one does not doubt
the sincerity of the words; the narrator *really* dislikes himself.

That is not the case with Dylan and that is due to his performance.
Unambiguous the emotion is not. We hear some assertiveness,
reproach and hurt, but self-hatred... no. Likewise, already the
second line lacks any hint of self-reflection. *"You were just a
painted face on a trip down Suicide Road"* is a good old-fashioned
Dylanesque put-down, completely in line with the vitriol of "Can
You Please Crawl Out Your Window?", "Positively 4th Street" and
"She's Your Lover Now", in line with the most vicious songs from
1965. The degrading *"you were just a painted face"* is a variant of
the equally villainous *"you just happened to be there, that's all"*
from "One Of Us Must Know (Sooner Or Later)", Suicide Road most
likely being a side street of Desolation Row.

And not at all in line with the rest of the songs on this album, *Planet
Waves*, an album on which, just as on predecessor *New Morning*,
life-affirmation, joys of love and contentment are predominant.

That missing connection to the rest of the songs on *Planet Waves* does not stand alone; text internally "Dirge" is not very coherent either. Apart from maybe "Never Say Goodbye", the other nine songs stay, verse line after verse line, decently true to one theme, varying on one message, staying neatly within the lines. "Forever Young" ties together fifteen interchangeable blessings, "You Angel You", the most wordy song of the album, repeats the same message six times in six stanzas, just like "Going, Going, Gone" does in four verses.

"Dirge", on the other hand, seems to be an exercise of free association and écriture automatique, in the vein of "Farewell Angelina" or "Tombstone Blues", the surrealist masterpieces from that artistic peak in the mid-1960s. Or, looking in the other direction, a taste of the songs Dylan will write for *Street Legal* a few years later, idiomatic processions like "Changing Of The Guards" and "No Time To Think".

Cold statistical data confirm this observation; "Dirge" is by far the most eloquent song of *Planet Waves*. Only "Wedding Song" has more words, but a much poorer ratio of words/unique words than "Dirge" (169 different words in a 275-word song).

Besides the similarity with the eloquence and the cryptic qualities of *Street Legal*, the lyrics of "Dirge" also have a matching "colour". Verses have a self-standing, aforistic power and have no further relationship with the previous or following line.

And they are beautiful lines, by the way. *"That hollow place where martyrs weep and angels play with sin"* and *"Like a slave in orbit, he's beaten 'til he's tame"* for example, or *"In this age of fiberglass I'm searching for a gem"*.

Especially the latter has such an atypical, clinical metaphor, at best recalling *"that trainload of fools bogged down in a magnetic field"* in "Señor" from - again - *Street Legal*, just like the next line (*"The crystal ball up on the wall hasn't shown me nothing yet"*) would fit in "Señor" instinctively, stylistically and intrinsically, but never in "Something There Is About You" or any other song on *Planet Waves*.

The conclusion that "Dirge" is such an odd duck out, provides new fuel to the admittedly apocryphal but amusing creation myth, as recorded by Clinton Heylin, among others. That story starts with the question of who this Martha is, from the original title "Dirge For Martha". She is then said to be a friend of Dylan's childhood friend Lou Kemp and would have triggered the creation of the song by saying to Dylan, after hearing the test recordings of "Forever Young": *"Are you getting mushy in your old age?"*

Everything indicates that "Dirge" indeed was written last-minute in the studio, towards the end of the recording sessions for *Planet Waves*. Guitarist Robbie Robertson, who improvises the tasteful Spanish ornaments, also remembers in his autobiography *Testimony* the rather spontaneous, unannounced birth:

"As Rob [*Fraboni, the producer*] and I were setting up to mix the album, Bob came into the control room and asked me to play on one more song. He sat at the piano and I picked up an acoustic Martin D- 28. He played through one verse to give me the flavor and then we cut it. This was "Dirge for Martha", and I think we only did one take. That session reminded me of late nights eight years earlier, Bob and me playing music in our hotel rooms."

Whether or not we owe "Dirge" to that empty-headed tease from some Martha, Robertson does not mention. It does not seem very credible, though. It is hard to imagine that the hardened Dylan after all these years full of poisonous reproaches and aggrieved criticism from nitwits, journalists and disappointed fans really could be affected by some clumsy insult from an insignificant girl.

Still, producer Fraboni also remembers a "Martha" incident and states how Dylan considers skipping the album highlight "Forever Young", which eventually leads to that strange compromise to put a second, less mushy version on the album.

So maybe it is true after all; perhaps the remarkable eruption "Dirge" *is* provoked by some silly lass.

The exegetes have a field day. Predictably often Sara is brought in and with the comfortable benefit of hindsight, a faction of both professional Dylanologists and excited bloggers analyse that the song is a run-up to *Blood On The Tracks*, to the bard's "Divorce Album". And solely regarding the style of the lyrics, there is some argument to be found; the same fragmented, associative labyrinth as "Up To Me", content likewise in minor, in farewell mode and true, the song is incomparable to the colour of the other songs on this album. But then again, the divorce from Sara is not until four years later and anyway, as those unimaginative Sara-exegetes have to admit, it is pretty impossible to squeeze the rest of the lyrics into that mould.

Most other exegetes also search for the key by framing the *you* from the opening line *I hate myself for loving you*. "Heroin" is a popular candidate, "Joan Baez" comes along (because of that one line *Heard your songs of freedom*), "a mistress", "fame", "Albert Grossman" and even "Edie Sedgwick". And subsequently, just like with the Sara-exegetes, it turns out to be impossible to fit more than two or three verse fragments into such an interpretation. "Fame" fits perhaps best.

It is not very surprising. Dylan does not write songs *à clef*, nor confessional songs, nor lyrics with a hidden, coded "actual" meaning. At best, he lets poetic expressions of private impressions twirl down into his lyrics. *I am about t sketch You a picture of what goes on around here sometimes. tho I don't understand too well myself what's really happening*, as Dylan writes in the liner notes of *Bringing It All Back Home* (1965) – "a sketchy rendering of personal impressions, without pretense of insight".

In that light, with that "key", one would indeed be tempted to trace and check off the images from "Dirge" with biographical knowledge of the man Dylan. "A face with a lot of make-up, about to commit suicide?" - check, Edie Sedgwick. And who is singing those *songs of freedom*? Joan Baez, obviously. Or perhaps Albert Grossman, who promises him financial and artistic freedom, if Dylan does what he is told. And *comme ça*, from every image, from every line of verse, a connection to a biographical reality from the author's life can be drawn.

The poverty of such an approach is the obviousness with which is taken for granted that the *I* from the song is identical with the author. The lyrics, however, do not give any reason for this assumption, apart from the banal fact that the lyrics are written by Dylan. But that same writer Dylan has repeatedly, and credibly, stated that the *I* from his songs is not automatically "me, Bob Dylan". *Je est un autre*, after all.

If we can let go of that starting point, the idée-fixe that the poet writes about himself, it also becomes easier to appreciate the song for what it is: a gripping jeremiade of a lost soul, an eloquent variant of a lamentation by Hank Williams ("Take These Chains From My Heart", for example) or a heart-rending blues by Robert Johnson like "Love In Vain" or "Kind Hearted Woman Blues"; songs about pitiful suckers who are in love with the wrong woman.

Despite all beauty, "Dirge" remains in the shadow. Dylan never plays the song; a further indication that he indeed just pulled the song from his hat, that November day in 1973. The established colleagues ignore the song too.

The living room versions of the fans on YouTube are without exception unbearable, as are those of the tribute bands and beyond that only a few professional artists from the second division are worth mentioning.

The jazz version of the Jamie Saft Trio, on the splendid album *Trouble* (2006), reduces "Dirge" to a desolate depression, but is spectacularly beautiful. The duo of Patches & Gretchen from

Minneapolis attracts attention because Dylan's *Desire* violinist Scarlett Rivera plays along, but their cover is not too distinctive. Gretchen is holding a rolling pin with an attached crib sheet for the lyrics, that has some entertainment value.

The most beautiful cover is on *In Between*, a 2010 album by Erik Truffaz. The Frenchman is originally a jazz trumpet player, and a particularly good one too, and makes excursions to hip hop, dance and rock. "Dirge" is a highlight on *In Between*. Guest singer Sophie Hunger is doing well, but overwhelming is the musical skill of the quartet. Beautifully arranged, sparse trumpet, great drumming and assertive, lyrical guitar. Superb Hammond organ, too.

Also, not the slightest trace of any self-hatred either, but what the heck.

The last call of the nightingale

The vein from which *Blood On The Tracks* flows is not yet empty, after the last recording day in Minneapolis. The themes Love & Loss, wrapped in words that suggest the intimacy and indiscretion of a diary, stylistically clear but impenetrable, partly due to the confusing play with Time and Pronouns ... the poet Dylan is still not bored. What is more, he thinks he has not yet put his finger on it, here on *Blood On The Tracks*.

> BD: Never until I got to *Blood On The Tracks* did I finally get a hold of what I needed to get a hold of and once I got hold of that, *Blood On The Tracks* wasn't it either, and neither was *Desire*. But *Street Legal* comes the closest to where my music is going, you know, for the rest of the time. It has to do with an illusion of time, I mean, what the songs are necessarily about is the illusions of time. Now, in the old days, they used to do it automatically, but it's like I had amnesia, all of a sudden in 1966. I couldn't remember how to do it. I tried to force-learn it, and I couldn't learn what I had been able to do naturally like *Highway 61 Revisited*. I mean, you can't sit down and write that consciously, I mean, because it has to do with the break-up of time.
>
> MD: Fragmentation, fragmentation's such an important part I guess in your art. I feel that.
>
> BD: You know, it's got, I mean, it's just... in four lines, in the first

four lines, it covers all you need to cover. It covers the past, present and future. I had to unlearn how to do that consciously because I learned in '75 that I was going to have to do it from now on... consciously; and those are the kinds of songs I wanted to write. The ones that do have the break-up of time, where there is no time, trying to make the focus as strong as a magnifying glass under the sun, you know. To do it consciously is a trick, you know and I did it on that... er... I did it on *Blood On The Tracks* for the first time, and I didn't know... I knew how to do it because it was a technique I learned, I actually had a teacher for it.

(interview Matt Damsker for *Philadelphia Evening,* September 1978)

Dylan tries to explain that the introduction to Norman Raeben, an old painter who gives idiosyncratic courses in New York, has led to a new insight into art. *Time* is a keyword, messing around with personal pronouns a means to suggest both synchronicity and a time mosaic. Dylan uses strong rhetoric to underline the influence of those Raeben lessons. In several interviews from '78 he brings it up, he does not shy away from the Big Words and sometimes seems to quote from The Hitchhiker's Guide To The Galaxy: "The old man had definite ideas on life and the universe and nature - all that matters." Not only does Raeben teach him to "consciously do what I felt unconsciously", he also teaches him how to grasp "ultimate realities" and he teaches him to actually, *really* see. It doesn't stop there. Dylan attributes guru-like powers to the old artist.

I had met magicians, but this guy Is more powerful than any magician I've ever met. He looked into you and told you what you were. (...) He was just some kind of guide, or something like that...

And perhaps most shocking is the claim that Norman Raeben even has marriage-destroying powers, according to a quote in Bert Cartright's article, "The Mysterious Norman Raeben":

> When Dylan looked back upon what happened during those two months, he came to believe that he was so transformed as to become a stranger to his wife:
> "It changed me. I went home after that and my wife never did understand me ever since that day. That's when our marriage started breaking up. She never knew what I was talking about, what I was thinking about. And I couldn't possibly explain it."

In an interview with Pete Oppel (*Dallas Morning News*, November '78) Dylan specifies the intensity of that period. For two months, five days a week, eight hours a day. Group course, together with "rich old women from Florida, a police officer, a bus driver and a lawyer". And a Norman Raeben who continuously talks, in seven languages, providing a sharp commentary on the painting attempts and the personalities of the participants, but "he put my mind and my hand and my eye together."

But then it is 2011 and Dylan's midlife crisis is over and when he looks back on those experiences he is sobered up. Following the *Asia Series*, an exhibition of Dylan's paintings, the official site dylan.com publishes the interview that originally is published in the catalog. It has been administered and written by the distinguished John Elderfield, former art curator of the Museum Of Modern Art in New York and professor at Princeton University. The erudite Elderfield naturally asks about Dylan's training, about those course days with Norman Raeben. What did you do there, and was that experience just as critical for your painting as it was for your music?

"Maybe what the old guy said about painting did have
something to do with the *Blood on the Tracks* record. But
basically, that whole period has been blown out of proportion
by people writing about that record. (...) He asked me why I
wanted to paint in the first place. I couldn't think of anything to
say, so I told him I wanted to replicate life, and he became quite
angry. Like, "What makes you think life needs to be replicated?"
He told me I was self-centered, and a real artist is anything but
that. After a couple of those sessions, I don't think I went back."

If you start calculating with the figures that Dylan mentions in that
Oppel interview, it will add up to about three hundred and sixty
hours, but in 2011 Dylan reduces that to "a couple of those
sessions". Even more surprising is the somewhat acidic accusation
that *others* are overstating the importance of that period. That is
really Mr. Dylan himself, who uses all those bold, mystifying words
to articulate the earth-shaking influence of Raeben. Just as it is
Dylan himself who trivializes it again almost forty years later.

In 1978, though, Dylan is still brimful of his Raeben experiences.
The divorce finalizing takes place in 1977, so both Dylan's art views
and his private worries are still the same as during the conception
of *Blood On The Tracks*. Rolling Thunder guitarist Steven Soles
confirms that in 1977 Dylan plays him "a whole bunch of songs"
that awkwardly, cold, harsh thematize a love break. Those songs
are never recorded, Dylan tells Robert Hilburn in May '78 (*Los
Angeles Times*). But the theme lingers on. It is not that difficult to
identify the songs that then, after Minneapolis, flow out of the
same vein: "Isis", "Sara", "We Better Talk This Over", "True Love
Tends To Forget" and - in terms of content, in any case - "Where
Are You Tonight? (Journey Through Dark Heat) ". Stylistically too,

those songs are largely a continuation of the "painting songs" on *Blood On The Tracks*; there is no linear narrative structure, the couplets illuminate mosaic-like, criss-cross, different scenes from an extinguishing love relationship. The poet omits, however, the trick to shake up personal pronouns. The *you* remains a *you*, the *I* remains an *I* and the *you* and *I* together are simply referred to as *we*.

Similarly, the *Desire*-outtake "Golden Loom" fits in well, but here the influence of William Blake dominates - the dark, highly symbolic metaphors and obscure references harmonize better with *Street Legal* songs such as "Changing Of The Guards" and "Señor (Tales Of Yankee Power)" then with the clear, light poetry of "Simple Twist Of Fate" and "You're Gonna Make Me Lonesome When You Go".

The song bridging the gap between the two albums Dylan writes too late to be released on *Blood On The Tracks* (and is rightly passed for the "intermediate album" *Desire*). It is also the only song from that period that could have perfected the perfect *Blood On The Tracks* even further: the lonely masterpiece "Abandoned Love".

15   Abandoned Love

It is a beautiful story, even though it is a true story. On a Thursday evening in July 1975, Dylan visits a performance by his old Greenwich Village buddy Ramblin' Jack Elliott, playing in the famous nightclub The Bitter End (which is briefly called The Other End in those days) on Bleecker Street. Elliott spots him, starts playing "With God On Our Side" and asks after a few lines if Bob might want to assist him. Pleasantly surprised, the hundred-headed audience sees Dylan taking the stage, grabbing a guitar and playing along with "Pretty Boy Floyd" and "How Long Blues".

He seems a little nervous, declines a first invitation to sing something, but then he exchanges his rattling guitar (he has troubles adjusting the capo) with Ramblin' Jack's, he starts to sing.

"After a couple of lines, we realized he was performing a new song," eyewitness Joe Kivak writes, "with each line getting even better than the last. The song was *Abandoned Love*, and it still is the most powerful performance I've ever heard."

Someone in the audience is so thoughtful as to make a sneaky recording that soon becomes extremely popular in bootleg circles, proving that Kivak hardly exaggerates; it is an enthusiastic, sparkling performance of an extremely beautiful song. It really must be the highlight of the upcoming LP.

A few weeks later, July 31, it is one of the last songs he records for that new LP, *Desire*, along with two other love songs: "Isis" and "Sara". In terms of lyrics, hardly anything has changed, but the sparkle has disappeared. The melody is of course still enchanting, the accompaniment at the high *Desire* level, the production crisp (unfortunately including that dated bathroom reverbeo in vocals and percussion), but compared to the live recording, an opacity has crept in, Dylan sings perfunctory. He dismisses the recording, which will appear on *Biograph* ten years later, for *Desire*. Perhaps the master also misses the pearl gloss of the gig on 3 July, or maybe he thinks a song about the end of a Great Love should have been on predecessor *Blood On The Tracks* - or is the content too intimate? After that one time he will never play it again, in any case.

That intimacy then would concern the candour about the end of the marriage with Sara, which indeed fairly effortlessly can be distilled from the lyrics. In the first half of the 70s, Dylan serves his followers and fans with a-typical openness. Songs like "Wedding Song", "Idiot Wind" and "You're Gonna Make Me Lonesome When You Go" are compared to earlier and later work remarkably undisguised, stripped of the usual misty ambiguity, and provide more than ever insight into the man's soul stirrings. Grist to the mill of the exegetes with less cryptanalytic talent, anyway.

"Abandoned Love" is a highlight in that subgenre. The underlying melancholy, regret, heartache and despair are clear, yet wrapped in Dylanesque metaphors and poetic emblems. The admiring witness of the first hour is right; already the first sentence is of great beauty. *I can hear the turning of the key* has a compelling rhythm, a strong evocative power and a catchy symbolic charge. And after this, sure enough, every line gets even better. The narrator does not spare himself; he is deceived by *the clown in me*, driven by misplaced vanity and now torn by the old and familiar conflict between head and heart. Sure, intellectually he understands it is over, but then: *my heart is a-tellin' me I love ya still*.

The biographical interpreter starts focusing the third time the protagonist professes his love in so many words: *my heart is telling me I love ya but you're strange*. We now know that the I person is thematizing the abandonment of a Great Love, a Great Love with whom he also has children - yes, this is really inspired by the upcoming former Mrs. Dylan. Who is, it must be said now, perhaps a bit *strange*.

The observation does not stand alone. On comparing various Sara observations from different sources, one can not escape the notion, besides all the respectful and affectionate descriptions: she indeed is a bit weird. Marianne Faithfull is not the only one who registers that she does not say much (in her highly humorous, touching and disconcerting autobiography from 1994) and describes her as *solid as marble*.

Levon Helm, the drummer of The Band, also senses something ethereal: *a Brazilian Madonna* (in his memoirs *This Wheel's On Fire*).

Sara connoisseur Joan Baez devotes quite a lot of words to her love rival in *And A Voice To Sing With*, and the sympathy that Baez seems to feel is predominant. Between the lines, however, she sprinkles asides and remarks that together do paint an image of quite a peculiar lady. More than once Sara's gaze is *quizzical* or *surprised*, often in combination with *foggy*. She is "too frail to be a mom," "ill-equipped to handle the practical matters of everyday," and Baez must help her with banal necessities such as finding towels and how to make coffee. However, Baez thinks Sara's eccentric, poetic phobia is enviable: Sara is afraid to stand on a bridge over still water. It even animates Joan to a song about her ("Still Waters At Night", on the disappointing *Gulf Winds*, 1976).

Likewise, in the Dylan songs which seem to sing Sara, the bard always puts in a few words that suggest that his adored one can be somewhat detached or vulnerable. She is a *Sphinx* and *hard to define* ("Sara"), she apparently has no wishes, because *she's got everything she needs* ("She Belongs To Me"), she is *like some raven with a broken wing* and *speaks like silence* ("Love Minus Zero / No Limit"), has a *ghostlike soul* and *a face like glass* ("Sad-Eyed Lady Of The Lowlands"). In any case, Sara inspires Dylan to his most beautiful love songs, that much is clear. And the sideways remarked eccentricities all fit well with that one subclause after that declaration of love, *I love ya but you're strange.*

However, the rejection of this little masterpiece may not be due to unease about the content. The text's style is unsteady, and that may bother the poet Dylan. The text-internal tension between clear, classic lines of verse like *Everybody's wearing a disguise* or clichéd pathos like *The treasure can't be found by men who search* on the one hand and symbol-charged, ambiguous imagery like *My patron saint is a-fighting with a ghost* or the breath-taking power of *Send out for St. John the Evangelist / All my friends are drunk, they can be dismissed* (rejected lines from the first version) on the other hand, almost tangibly illustrates the crossroads on which the poet is now standing. It is a final eruption of the lucid poetry on *Blood On The Tracks* and a first glance at the heavy, hermetic lyricism of *Street Legal*.

After the release of that underwhelming studio recording from July '75 on the sales success *Biograph* (1985), "Abandoned Love" also penetrates into the repertoire of eager colleagues. The Everly Brothers act fast (on *Born Yesterday*, 1985) with a rather corny, Celtic coloured version. It sounds more authentic with the full-blooded Irishman Séan Keane (*All Heart No Roses*, 1994), but the drabness is just as intolerable. The interpretation by Alistair Moock is already easier to digest, although his singing style pushes the song in the direction of "Streets Of London".

George Harrison chooses (or: most likely only knows) the studio version's opening line *I can <u>hear</u> the turning of the key*, and delivers a beautifully arranged cover - but no; old George's voice has never been wild or mercury, only thin, unfortunately. And the 80s sauce over the production does not do much good either. By the way, Harrison records it in the fall of 1984, well before *Biograph*'s release; presumably his friend Dylan has pointed out to him the existence of the song.

The most beautiful covers are the various live versions from the Californian Chuck Prophet, the master guitarist and singer-songwriter who never really breaks through. Prophet produces distinctive, quirky Dylan covers (his "From A Buick 6" is a highlight), but refrains himself with "Abandoned Love", in a faithful, loving, driving arrangement that, in part due to the guitar tsunami, towers high over the other covers.

Still, to the maestro's embryonic, original pub recording from July '75 no one comes close - not even Dylan himself.

Sundown, yellow moon

In November 2016, best-selling author (*Dress Gray*) and the *Village Voice*'s staff writer with the Most Impressive Name, Lucian K. Truscott IV, writes down one of his most cherished memories, from the summer of '74. He then lives in a $ 200 loft on the fourth floor on 124 West Houston Street, Manhattan, on the edge of Soho. When signing the lease three years earlier, the landlord has already told him that Bob Dylan is renting a rehearsal room on the first floor. That does not impress Truscott too much; he knows that Dylan has a house around the corner on MacDougal Street, but also that he is rarely in New York in those years. Dylan restlessly seeks rest, as Truscott understands. From Woodstock to Santa Fe to Malibu. At the same time, Dylan is so much *part of the fabric of the city* that one never has the feeling that he is not there.

Occasionally then Dylan actually is in New York and sometimes Truscott hears him making music. Dylan's studio is separated from the hallway only by a plaster wall, so it is easy to hear. Especially since he has the piano against that wall, as Truscott happens to know, as he once helped him bringing in amplifiers and such.

One day, when Truscott sees a folding chair lying among some trash on the sidewalk, he brings it up and hides it under the stairs, against Dylan's wall. Sitting there, he can secretly listen in and that is how he hears him working in that summer of '74 "on something extraordinary": the songs that will become *Blood On The Tracks*.

> Dylan had always had a way of distilling being young and living in New York City. His songs piled up images, metaphors, hints about his life. Trying to read into them, we could also read who we were. But this was something entirely different. This was Dylan without the cloak of lyrical mystery. This was how he felt unfettered, who he saw looking in the mirror. He was doing in public something we had all gone through in private — breaking up with a lover, bleeding anger and regret, love and loss, and pain. Lots and lots of pain.

Truscott spends quite some time on his folding chair under the stairs, and the highlight is yet to come. That takes place one afternoon, as he walks down the stairs and hears Dylan working on a new song on the piano.

> I got out my folding chair and listened. He was writing his midlife masterpiece, "Idiot Wind." He had that melody down, with its mix of wistfulness and acid resentment, but he was having a hell of a time with the lyrics. He would sing a verse and, dissatisfied, bang his fists on the keyboard. Then he'd take a moment and start again.

He knocked out the refrain quickly, his anger bubbling up in raw bile. "Idiot wind, blowing every time you move your teeth." Vicious stuff. I sat and listened as he struggled with the reckoning, that there wasn't just one idiot to blame.

> *Idiot wind*
> *Blowing through the buttons of our coats*
> *Blowing through the letters that we wrote*

(*Bang bang* on the keyboard...another pass...*bang bang*...what next?)

> *Blowing through the dust upon our shelves*

Then the banging stopped, and — so quietly I could barely hear him through the thin wall — he caressed the keys as he wrote the final lines of the song:

> *We're idiots, babe*
> *It's a wonder we can even feed ourselves.*

Utterly enviable, and Truscott does have more of those Dylan moments in the following months. Around the corner is *The Bitter End*, where Dylan sometimes just steps onto the stage and where he hears and sees him play that unique, superior "Abandonded Love", where he introduces his then unknown friend Patti Smith to the bard. And when Dylan hears that Truscott has been invited to the annual Christmas party of Norman Mailer, he likes to come along, so the journalist witnesses "the two most famous Jews in America" meet for the first time.

But those hours under the stairs, listening to the creation of *Blood On The Tracks*, is the memory he truly cherishes, obviously.

Truscott is not the only one for whom *Blood On The Tracks* somehow is a milestone. Between 2014 and 2016, around the 40th anniversary of Dylan's midlife masterpiece, much attention is paid to the album and so Glenn Berger gets all the space in the *Esquire* of September 17, 2014 - because it is 40 years after the New York recording sessions - to tell the Dylan story from his captivating autobiography *Never Say No To A Rockstar* (2016).

Berger tells with charming modesty how he was a trainee at Phil Ramone at the time, how instructive it was to be rammed, squeezed or ignored every day by Ramone, but he is proud to say: "I am the only person alive, besides the man himself, who witnessed all of those sessions."

His own role is not too spectacular. Glenn is an eighteen-year-old boy and only a *schlepper*, a coolie. Occasionally, by order of the boss, pressing a button, preparing a microphone, changing tapes, that kind of work. Dylan hardly notices him and growls at him at best.

It doesn't matter, Berger is there to learn and enjoys the knowledge that he is working on a mythical album in pop history. But afterwards he is secretly a bit disappointed that his name is not mentioned in the credits.

Forty years later he even begins to quietly wonder whether it is actually entirely true, or whether he just made up a memory. After all, there is no evidence at all. Or is there? His name should be mentioned on the so-called take sheets, which also record who is working in the studio. Quickly, Glenn googles. There are some major Dylan freaks out there, he knows. And indeed: one Michael Krosgaard has thrown it all on the net. Glenn Berger impatiently scrolls down and yes indeed, there it is:

> *Engineers: Phil & Lenn*

He can laugh about it.

When asked what he learned from those sessions with Ramone and Dylan, Berger gets poetic:

> I did come to understand that artists are not supposed to be nice. They're on a mission from beyond. They go down, deeper into themselves than any of us dare, go through Hell on the journey, steal the sacred fire, and bring it up to share with the rest of us. [...] *Blood on the Tracks*. Dylan poured his guts into these songs and that's why they will long endure. He had access to the source in a way that I can only sweetly envy. I can see the brilliance, but it eludes my grasp like an eggshell in the bowl.
>
> I know it's Dylan's blood on those tracks and that's what makes them great. But I take some small measure of solace for my pain and limitations by telling myself that along with his blood, there is also a little bit of mine.

In his autobiography, chapter 5, or "Track Five", as he calls it, is entirely devoted to the recording sessions for *Blood On The Tracks*. His story broadly confirms, but with much more details and psychological depth, the bizarre working method of Dylan. This talent is traceable; After twenty years, Berger said goodbye to the music business and he now works as a psychiatrist in Manhattan. However, as a young schlepper he already had an eye for the bewilderment, desperation and humiliation of session musicians who have to follow the inimitable Dylan during those completely unstructured recording sessions in 1974. The silent indignation and the unjustified but understandable embarrassment of the failing musicians who are discarded with a single hand gesture from the master, until ultimately only bass player Tony Brown is left... the stories have been told before, by Ramone, by Weissberg, by Andy Gill, but not by an eyewitness with such a sharp power of observation and the talent to express it.

Touching is also his dismay at the revelation that his hero Dylan is such a nasty guy. After a breath-taking take of "Idiot Wind", Dylan enters the control room and snarls sarcastically: "Was that since-e-e-re enough?"

> He'd murdered his musicians with the aplomb of a psychopath; he recorded his album sloppily in a day and then did it again two times more, and now this? Was it fucking *sincere* enough? I was ready to puke. [...] The egotistical pricks I'd indulged were all good fun compared to this.

But it is inevitable, he realizes years later. The greatest art is created by loners, by artists who knowingly and deliberately turn away from social conventions. And the experience of being an eyewitness to the creation of a masterpiece by a genius is not tarnished thereby:

> I could feel the burn of creation from the other side of the glass. Dylan. Songs were bursting out of him like lava spewing from a volcano. He was mainlined to the source. What they call genius. I saw him write a song's lyrics on a yellow legal pad like he was taking dictation, he couldn't write fast enough. And the songs would rewrite themselves as he sang them. Take 1 would have a verse that sounded so good you could gasp with revelation, and then he'd do Take 2 and it would blow away the last one like so much ash after a fire.

The last word is for Kevin Odegaard, who is interviewed by Kate Nelson in January 2018 for Artful Living. Odegaard has a right to a say; he plays the guitar on all Minneapolis recordings, contributes significantly to the indestructible beauty of "Tangled Up In Blue" and has written with Andy Gill the beautiful, insightful and thorough work *A Simple Twist Of Fate: Bob Dylan And The Making Of Blood on The Tracks*. Apparently, Odegaard's sources have not dried up since the publication of that book (2004), because he comes up with new facts in the interview. For example about the origin of the re-recordings in Minneapolis.

> I've heard a few different versions. The legend I choose to believe is that Norio Ohga, the president of Sony at the time, was developing a new device called the Walkman. Bob was listening over and over again to the New York City recording sessions on his Walkman and brought it home for the holidays.

Only a small detail, but in his own book and in all other stories it is always *acetates* that Ramone quickly had made for Dylan - a Walkman prototype is never mentioned.

An important part of the review then repeats anecdotes and facts that we all know from the book, but striking again is Odegaard's summary thereof. Striking, because the perceptive Odegaard registers almost the same artist's characteristic in Minneapolis as schlepper Glenn Berger does in New York:

> And what I got by doing the enormous amount of digging that I did is that you could just keep digging forever and never get to the bottom of Bob Dylan — because there's no bottom there. He's a vessel. He's a channel. He's a conduit.
>
> So it was a vacant experience for me in one sense, because I never got to the spiritual heart of that. And Bob didn't participate

in the writing of the book. He didn't want to deal with the fact that Blood on the Tracks might have been about his divorce. So he made up a story about it being about a series of Chekhov plays. He didn't want to address it, even though his own children later said, "That's my mom and dad talking on that album. That's them."

But the more digging I did, the more I realized this is part of the nature of genius. A genius is plugged into something even he doesn't understand. And that's true of Bob. When he gives speeches, it's like one of his songs. They are these brilliant, stream-of-consciousness rants about everything coming through his mind at the moment.

Plausible. In any case, more intelligent than Odegaard's title explanation; because in "Idiot Wind" the phrase *blood on your saddle* comes by, Dylan called the album *Blood On The Tracks*.

Sources

Well, I investigated all the books in the library
Ninety percent of 'em gotta be burned away

Dylan:

- *Lyrics 1962 - 2001* (2004)
- www.bobdylan.com
- *Chronicles* (2004)
- *Blood On The Tracks* (1975)
- *Theme Time Radio Hour* (2006-08)

Interview fragments (in addition to the titles mentioned):

- *Every Mind Polluting Word* (collected interviews, 2006)
- *Rolling Stone* (interview Sept 7, 2006)
- *Life with Bob Dylan* (Uncut interviews,1989-2006)
- *Leonard Cohen Makes It Darker,* The New Yorker Oct 17, 2016

On Dylan (in addition to the titles mentioned):

- *Liner notes* Blood On The Tracks, Pete Hamill, 1975
- *Liner notes* Trouble No More, Amanda Petrusisch, 2017
- *Revolution in the Air* - Clinton Heylin, 2009
- *Still On The Road* - Clinton Heylin, 2010
- *Down The Highway* - Howard Sounes, 2001
- *Bob Dylan In America* - Sean Wilentz, 2010

- *Time Out Of Mind* - Ian Bell, 2013
- *No Direction Home* - Robert Shelton, 1986
- *Visions Of Sin* - Christopher Ricks, 2003
- *Bob Dylan Writings, 1968-2010* - Greil Marcus, 2010
- *Liner notes* Biograph - Cameron Crowe, 1985
- bjorner.com
- bobdylaninnederland.blogspot.nl
- expectingrain.com
- *Untold Dylan,*bob-dylan.org.uk

Miscellaneous (in addition to the titles mentioned):

- *De Kellnerin* – Herman Pieter de Boer, 1977
- *Men In Black II,* Barry Sonnenfeld, 2002
- *Backstage Passes And Backstabbing Bastards* - Al Kooper, 1998
- *A Simple Twist Of Fate* - Andy Gill en Kevin Odegard, 2005
- *Why Dylan Matters* – Richard F. Thomas, 2017
- *And A Voice To Sing With* - Joan Baez, 1987
- *Faithfull; An Autobiography* - with David Dalton, 1994
- *Testimony,* Robbie Robertson, 2016
- *This Wheel's On Fire,* Levon Helm, 1993
- *Making Music – The Scenes Behind The Music,* Phil Ramone and Charles L. Granata, 2007
- *Never Say No To A Rock Star,* Glenn Berger, 2016
- *Bible,* various translations. Mainly King James

Notes

This book is the English translation of the Dutch book *Blood On The Tracks - Dylans meesterwerk in blauw*, published by Brave New Books in November 2018 (ISBN 9789402179682)

In 2018 and 2019, fifteen of these twenty-one articles were already published on the British site *Untold Dylan*.

Thanks

Tom Willems, from *bobdylaninnederland.blogspot.nl* - the mercury Dylan blog, author of *Dylan & The Beats,* 2018

Martin Bierens - dear old Bobhead, from Utrecht to Amsterdam to Dornbirn to Stadskanaal to Tilburg to Bielefeld

Tony Attwood - webmaster of *Untold Dylan,* the place where it's always safe and warm

Printed in Great Britain
by Amazon

83808050R00099